Living with Multiple Sclerosis
A Wellness Approach

Living with Multiple Sclerosis
A Wellness Approach

George H. Kraft, M.D., MS

Professor, Rehabilitation Medicine
University of Washington
Director, Multiple Sclerosis Clinical Center
University of Washington Medical Center
Seattle, Washington

Marci Catanzaro, R.N., C.S

Gerontological Nurse Practitioner
Primary Health Care Associates
Seattle, Washington

demos vermande

Demos Vermande, 386 Park Avenue South, New York, New York 10016

© 1996 by Demos Vermande. All rights reserved. This book is protected by copyright. No part of it may be reproduced, stored in a retrieval system, or transmitted in any form or by any means, electronic, mechanical, photocopying, recording, or otherwise, without the prior written permission of the publisher.

Library of Congress Cataloging-in-Publication Data
Kraft, George H.
    Living with multiple sclerosis : a wellness approach / George H.
Kraft, Marci Catanzaro.
        p.   cm.
    Includes index.
    ISBN 1-888799-00-5 (softcover)
    1. Multiple sclerosis—Popular works.   I. Catanzaro, Marci.
    II. Title.
    RC377.K73   1996
    362 1'96834—dc20   96-4584
                                                            CIP

Made in the United States of America

Acknowledgments

Special credit and thanks to Pam Cavallo, Director of the Client & Community Services Department, for creating and nurturing the national teleconference program, and to Cindee McLaughlin, Senior Services Consultant, for her ongoing assistance with this project. A special thank you to our co-sponsor, Paralyzed Veterans of America, and to Berlex Laboratories and the Jimmie Heuga Center for their educational grants to support the teleconference.

Contents

Foreword

How can someone who has a chronic disease like multiple sclerosis also be healthy? The answer is by choosing behaviors that promote health. The World Health Organization views health as the optimal level of function and well-being within the possible limitations imposed by a physical or mental impairment. As multiple sclerosis fluctuates or even progresses, the overall physical and emotional capacity can be nurtured, and improvement achieved within realistic goals. This broad and positive approach to health is also conceptualized as "wellness," with emphasis on those areas within our control, those opportunities to make thoughtful and informed choices to enhance our function, attitudes, and general sense of well-being. This approach not only has implications for the present, but can also impact long-term health. Cardiovascular fitness feels good today, but also reduces risk of heart attacks and stroke in later years. In order to choose wisely, it is necessary to be informed of the ramifications of various behaviors and activities. This book addresses the overall area of choices for wellness and related issues.

The material presented in this book is adapted from the question and answer portion of a national teleconference, produced by the National Multiple Sclerosis Society. A primary function of the Society is to provide information about multiple sclerosis (MS) to a variety of audiences, including people with MS, their families, health professionals, employers, the general public. Although "Taking Control: Options to Maximize Your Health" was directed at people with MS, participants were present from all of these groups, totaling over 8,000 at more than 450 sites across the country. Ten separate programs were held to accommodate questions from each site. A videotape of people with MS and Drs. Catanzaro and Kraft was first shown, followed by the question and answer component. Participants have consistently praised the Society's national teleconference program, and "Taking Control: Options to Maximize Your Health" won a silver national Health Information Award.

I am delighted that the invaluable information provided by Drs. Catanzaro and Kraft to our teleconference participants can be shared with an even wider audience. It is critical for people with MS to maximize their health by reaching for even higher levels of physical and emotional wellness.

Nancy J. Holland, Ed.D.
Vice President
National Multiple Sclerosis Society
Client & Community Services

Preface

This book is an outgrowth of questions raised by people with multiple sclerosis (MS), their family members, and friends. Each day scientists learn more about the mechanisms that cause MS, ways of slowing the progression of the disease, and how to treat its symptoms. Answers to the questions raised will evolve over time and will become more complete. The value of a question and answer book, such as this one, is that the questions often remain the same. Those questions can serve as a study guide to learning more about MS. Ask these questions over and over as research produces greater insight and more complete answers. Ask questions of your health care provider, speakers at multiple sclerosis educational programs, the staff at the National Multiple Sclerosis Society, and anyone else whom you believe may have new answers to old questions. These questions may serve to stimulate your thinking and raise other questions about causes and treatment of MS and the management of symptoms.

No matter what new information is forthcoming about the causes and treatments of MS, successful living with this progressive neurologic disease depends on the person with disease. Taking control of your life in order to maximize your health is essential for each of us, whether or not we have MS. This book suggests some avenues for optimizing your health through exercise, nutrition, and emotional health. Use it as a jumping off point for putting together your own individualized program of wellness. Everyone needs a wellness program that addresses his or her individualized strengths and weaknesses. Consult your health care providers, nutritionist, therapist, and counselors. You are the most important person in maintaining your wellness.

CAUSE AND COURSE OF
MULTIPLE SCLEROSIS

The cause of multiple sclerosis still eludes scientists, although every year more information about the cause is obtained. We do know many things about its etiology (cause) from epidemiologic and laboratory studies. For example, we know that MS is more common in the northern parts of the northern hemisphere and southern parts of the southern hemisphere. It is much less common in tropical climates. We also know that peoples from certain genetic backgrounds have a much higher incidence of MS than others. For example, MS is far more common in people of northern European than African stock. Evidence points to the fact that it is where children grow up and spend the first half of the teen years—rather than where they live when the symptoms occur—that is associated with the likelihood of getting MS. Viral etiologies are suspected, but none has yet been proven. A popular line of thinking is that a specific virus does not set off the abnormal function of the immune system attacking myelin, but rather a frequent association with many childhood viruses that triggers an attack much later.

Some years ago, before the development of magnetic resonance imaging (MRI) and evoked potentials (EP) such as visual, somatosensory, and brain stem evoked potentials, diagnosis was based on specific characteristics of the disease course. Abnormalities in several parts of the nervous system occurring over a period of time had to occur before the diagnosis could be made. More recently, the MRI, EPs, and newer tests such as magnetic resonance spectroscopy are enhancing the ability of clinicians to make the diagnosis early. In previous years, it was not uncommon for a person to wait two or more years after the first symptoms for a diagnosis to be made. With the new diagnostic tools, the diagnosis may now be made within days after the first onset of symptoms.

Although the course of MS is very variable, about 70 percent of people with the disease start with a relapsing and remitting course in which the remissions are complete and long in the early phases. At some point, exacerbations occur more frequently and remissions are less complete. This course eventually tends to transform into what is known as a secondary progressive form, where there is a relatively steady worsening without the earlier fluctuations. Perhaps 5 to 10 percent of the patients have a course that is progressive from onset (primary progressive MS). These patients tend to have a worse prognosis. Commonly, they are older men. Lastly, there is a benign form of the disease in which people may have a lifetime without significant problems, having only enough symptomatology for the diagnosis to be made. It is unclear how many people have this form of MS; there may actually be more than medical practitioners suspect, since symptomatology is minimal throughout the lives of most of these people.

Disease Distribution

Q: Why is multiple sclerosis more prevalent in the North?

A: We know that there is a higher prevalence of MS between 40°
and 60° latitude north. We also know that where people are born
and reared as children is more predictive of who gets MS than where
they are living at the time symptoms appear. Although we do not know
the reason for sure, many scientists suspect that this may relate to
a higher incidence in northern latitudes of children playing together inside—and getting more viral infections. Also, there is a genetic
component: people of Northern European countries have a higher
incidence of MS, and more of these people live in the North.

Q: Is multiple sclerosis more common in women?

A: Yes. In fact, MS is about twice as common in women as in men.
We do not know why that is so but we do know that other autoimmune diseases are also more common in women.

Q: Do children get MS?

A: Yes, there are verified cases of MS in school-aged children. The disease most commonly has an onset between the ages of fifteen and fifty
years. Often people who are older when they are diagnosed had their
first symptoms many years before.

Q: Does MS affect one socioeconomic class more than another?

A: In the United States it appears that the disease is more common in higher socioeconomic groups. It has been suggested that MS may be caused by a slow-acting virus. Perhaps children who live in poverty are exposed to more viruses in infancy, offering them some form of immune protection, which decreases their chances of developing MS later. Another possible explanation is that higher socioeconomic groups have better access to health care and are more likely to seek health care and diagnosis of neurologic symptoms. But this is all speculation; the true reason is not known.

Cause of Multiple Sclerosis

Q: Is MS caused by something in the environment?

A: The cause of MS remains unknown. Various environmental factors, including viruses and toxins such as dental amalgam and organic solvents, have been suggested as possible causes, although there is absolutely no evidence for most such factors. Some studies have suggested that viral exposure in childhood may increase the likelihood of developing MS. Many viruses have been studied, but none of them alone has been demonstrated to play a key role in the etiology of the disease. No connection has been established between chemicals or toxins and the development of MS.

Q: Is MS a genetically inherited disease?

A: Some diseases, such as Duchenne's muscular dystrophy, are genetically inherited by the Mendelian rules taught in high school biology. Multiple sclerosis is much more complex. The disease tends to occur more frequently in families than in the general population, but technically it is not considered a genetically inherited disease. People with certain genetic markers are more likely to develop MS than people with other genetic markers. For example, people of Scandinavian origin are much more likely to develop MS than those of African origin. Thus there is probably a genetic "predisposition" to MS that is related to how the body's immune system works. Genes alone do not determine who gets MS—some event must trigger the onset of the disease. We know from the study of identical twins, who have exactly the same genetic makeup, that it is possible for only one twin to develop MS, although the likelihood of a second twin developing the disease is greater than for siblings who are nonidentical.

Q: Is there a genetic test specific to multiple sclerosis?

A: No, there is no genetic test for MS. A variety of genetic markers have been associated with MS. Not everyone with the disease has these markers, and not everyone who has these markers develops MS.

Q: How is the immune system related to MS?

A: The immune system is incredibly complex. Entire books have been written about it and yet there is much to be learned. Very simply, the T-lymphocytes (a type of white blood cell) regulate the invasion of viruses and resist bacterial invasion and malignant cell changes. For reasons that we do not understand, the T-lymphocytes play a key role in the destruction of myelin, behaving as if myelin were a foreign substance. Abnormal levels of killer T cells and suppressor T cells have been found in the blood and spinal fluid of people with MS, especially during an exacerbation.

Q: What is the relationship between AIDS and MS?

A: Both diseases involve the immune system. Beyond that there is no similarity. Basic research on how the immune system works and things that alter its function will contribute to our understanding of MS as well as other diseases affecting the immune system.

Diagnosis

Q: What is required by most doctors to give a confirmed diagnosis of MS?

A: The diagnosis of MS continues to present challenges, although it is much easier than it was ten to fifteen years ago. The name *multiple sclerosis* answers what is necessary to make a diagnosis: there must be at least two areas of myelin destruction (sclerosis) present in the central nervous system (brain and spinal cord). In other words, more than one area of the brain or spinal cord must be involved in the disease process. Newer diagnostic techniques such as evoked potential studies and MRI scans can help to identify areas of damaged myelin before they produce symptoms. In years past, the diagnosis of definite multiple sclerosis may have taken a long time. That is why some people were initially told they "probably" or "possibly" had multiple sclerosis.

Q: Are spinal fluid analysis and biopsies necessary to diagnosis MS?

A: Structural changes in the central nervous system can be seen on MRI scans, and physiologic changes in nerve conduction can be measured by visual, somatosensory, and brain stem evoked potentials. Spinal fluid analysis is useful to identify changes in protein content that are associated with MS. A biopsy would only be required if there were an abnormal growth that might be a tumor. These invasive tests have largely been replaced with MRI and evoked potential tests.

Q: How long does it take for MS to appear on an MRI?

A: Typically, by the time a person has the first symptoms of MS, an MRI will identify multiple lesions. However, in approximately five to seven percent of people with MS, the initial lesions are in the spinal cord—usually the cervical region—and not in the brain. Therefore, the MRI must be taken of the most likely affected portion of the CNS.

Q: What other disorders mimic MS?

A: Any abnormality of the brain or spinal cord can cause symptoms similar to those of MS. Vascular problems, such as small strokes, can mimic MS. Metabolic disorders such as vitamin B deficiencies or diabetes mellitus can affect the central nervous system. Nerves can be trapped between muscles or bones and produce symptoms of numbness, tingling, and weakness. Infections, tumors, and collagen diseases such as lupus erythematosus can produce a clinical picture that looks like MS. Other neurologic diseases like amyotrophic lateral sclerosis (ALS) can also be confused with MS.

Q: Should people diagnosed with MS before evoked potentials and magnetic resonance imaging (MRI) were available have these tests?

A: The advent of new technology has made the diagnosis of MS easier and faster. If you have already been diagnosed with definite MS based on strict clinical criteria, there is no need to apply this new technology to confirm the diagnosis. However, if your diagnosis is "probable" or "possible" MS, you may want to have these newer tests. Also, you may want these tests if there was reason to suspect that you had developed another disorder of the nervous system. For example, people with MS can also get a herniated disc or have a stroke.

Q: Why are more cases of MS are being diagnosed now than in years before?

A: Several factors contribute to the apparently increased incidence of MS. First, we now have much more sophisticated diagnostic capabilities.

The MRI scan and electrophysiologic tests help to identify demyelinated areas in the brain and spinal cord so that physicians can be more certain of the diagnosis earlier in the course of the disease. Second, there was a long period in the history of medicine when nothing could be done to alter the course of MS, so many people were not told their diagnosis. Now that we have drugs such as beta interferon that reduce the frequency of exacerbations in MS, and many ways to treat the symptoms of MS, physicians are much more likely to tell people that they have MS.

Disease Course

Q: How do you know whether you have the relapsing-remitting or progressive type of MS?

A: In general, an exacerbating and remitting course of MS is just that—symptoms flare-up or worsen or new symptoms appear and then get at least somewhat better. In primary or secondary progressive MS, the disease simply moves steadily ahead and the person's condition continues to worsen. About 70 percent of people with MS start out having exacerbating and remitting disease. Later in the course of their disease, remissions become less complete and there is more and more residual disability. After many years, people often find that they no longer have the exacerbations and remissions, and the disease either stabilizes or follows a secondary progressive course.

Q: Why do remissions occur?

A: When myelin is destroyed, a local reaction takes place, much like what you see when you injure your skin. The surrounding area becomes inflamed and swollen, and nerve conduction may be blocked. This inflammation gradually disappears. As the inflammatory response around an affected area diminishes, symptoms become less severe. A great deal of myelin needs to be damaged and replaced by scar tissue before symptoms become permanent.

Q: What can trigger an exacerbation?

A: The unpredictable nature of MS causes us to search for something that causes a worsening of symptoms. Emotional stress, immunizations, infections and other illnesses, changes in the weather, and trauma have all been credited with causing MS exacerbations. The scientific evidence is variable, however, that these factors consistently cause problems for people with MS. People with MS can become worse with fever brought on by infection—often urinary tract infection. Symptoms improve with successful treatment of the infection. Many call this a "pseudo-exacerbation."

Q: Can poor nutrition trigger an episode?

A: Poor nutrition has many long-term effects. However, it is probably not something directly associated with an exacerbation of MS.

Q: Does natural adrenalin associated with stress prevent exacerbations?

A: When we are under a lot of stress, our bodies normally produce high levels of adrenal corticoids, natural substances similar to the drugs used to treat exacerbations of MS. People with MS often have no problems during high stress periods. When the stress is over, however, a rapid decrease in cortisol levels occurs and some people have an exacerbation.

Q: What wellness therapies are most likely to bring about a remission?

A: Unfortunately, we do not understand enough about the basic pathophysiology of exacerbations and remissions to answer that question. Certainly things like keeping yourself in optimal health are a critical part of dealing with MS. Eating a well-balanced diet, getting an adequate amount of sleep, and avoiding infectious diseases are all important. Bladder or lung infections can raise body temperature and make symptoms temporarily worse, but there is no evidence that they affect the long-term course of MS.

Q: Can exercise change the course of MS?

A: Exercise in and of itself does not alter the course of MS. However, evidence has shown that both resistive exercise (lifting weights) and aerobic exercise (e.g., exercise bicycle) can produce some degree of positive benefit in persons with MS, just as they do in healthy people. It is important that a person with MS try to keep body temperature from rising too much while exercising.

Q: Are there specific factors that determine how fast MS will progress?

A: The best we have are some "guesstimates" as to the future. Certain onset patterns can help to predict where MS will be five, ten, or fifteen years later. In general, those who have little disability five years after onset have a better long-term prognosis than those who are fairly disabled at that time. Persons whose MS started with ataxia (movement problems or tremor) or weakness tend to have a poorer prognosis than do people whose MS started with sensory symptoms. Also, an absence of initial remission is a poor prognostic sign.

SYMPTOM MANAGEMENT

It is said that we are known by the company we keep. Multiple sclerosis is a disease known by its symptoms.

A person with MS does not typically think of the demyelination in central nervous tissue that occurs, but rather thinks of the symptoms that these "short circuits" produce. A person with MS will more likely think about weakness, fatigue, tingling, or spasticity. Because MS occurs at various sites in the brain and spinal cord, the longer the pathway that the nerve impulse must take, the more likely that nerve function will be interrupted and symptoms will occur. For example, the nerves to the bladder come from the spinal cord just below the nerves to the lower legs. Because of their length from the brain, these two areas, then, have the highest probability of being affected by one or more MS plaques as the impulses descend from the brain through the spinal cord. People with MS know the frequency of symptoms in these areas.

Although the "bad news" is that the bladder and lower legs are frequently affected in people with MS, the "good news" is that there are many things that can be done about these symptoms. Various types of medications and treatments are useful for people with bladder dysfunction, and exercise and bracing can help people with ankle and foot weakness.

Because of the interruption in the central nervous system, other symptoms such as fatigue, balance problems, temperature sensitivity, and muscle spasms can also occur. Even though the damaged nerves causing these problems cannot be repaired, there are things that can be done, both medically and nonmedically, to alleviate many of the symptoms produced by interruption of these nerve pathways. Similar types of nerve dysfunction can also affect the sensory pathways and produce various types of pain.

There are many therapies, which will be discussed in this and the next three chapters (Wellness Management, Emotional Health, and Disease Treatments), that can help people having problems caused by these interrupted nerve pathways. It should also be remembered that MS does not necessarily occur in isolation. People with MS can develop other problems, such as arthritis in the joints, which may inter-react with the symptoms of MS to make management very difficult. In this chapter we answer some questions on this matter as well.

Balance

Q: What can be done to improve balance and coordination?

A: A physical therapist can work with someone experiencing problems with balance. Some exercises, such as Frenkel's repetitive placement exercises, will improve balance and coordination to some degree.

Q: What treatments or strategies can be used for treatment of dizziness or vertigo?

A: Dizziness or vertigo may be caused by demyelination of parts of the brain that are responsible for balance and coordination. Sometimes a plaque on the floor of the fluid-filled spaces in the brain (ventricles) can cause dizziness. These symptoms are very difficult to treat. Sometimes dizziness and vertigo are related to position, and the person can learn to get up slowly and avoid rapid movements of the head. Medications to treat vertigo are sometimes helpful. Special attention must be paid to drugs used to treat other symptoms of MS and that have effects on the brain that may contribute to feelings of light-headedness and dizziness. One must be sure that the symptoms are not side effects of some other medications.

Bladder and Bowel

Q: What causes bladder control problems in some people with MS?

A: Bladder problems are fairly common and are caused by demyelination in parts of the brain or spinal cord. Different types of bladder problems can occur in MS. One type occurs when the bladder does not empty completely, because the simultaneous bladder contraction and sphincter relaxation that allows urine to be expelled does not function as it should. This is known as bladder "dyssynergia." A second type of problem occurs when the bladder is hyperactive and contracts in response to a small amount of urine. Rarely is the problem due only to a lack of strength of bladder contraction, which results in some urine remaining in the bladder. When MS damages more than one area of the brain or spinal cord, the person can have a combination of problems.

Q: How do you know what kind of bladder problem MS is causing?

A: It is not always possible to tell the kind of bladder dysfunction by signs and symptoms only. The end result of a bladder that does not empty completely, or one that empties too often, is urinary frequency and incontinence. It is important to have the problem assessed by someone who understands the neurologic causes of bladder dysfunction. Sometimes people with MS have a combination of problems with the urinary sphincter and bladder contraction.

Q: What diagnostic tests need to be done to assess bladder problems?

A: Measuring the amount of urine left in the bladder after a person empties his/her bladder (post-voiding residual) will show if the bladder is emptying completely. A bladder filling test (cystometrogram) can show how sensitive the bladder is to stretching as it fills and the person's ability to suppress the urge to void. Sometimes it is necessary to also study the sphincter muscles with electromyography. A cystoscopy is necessary when bladder stones or pathology of the bladder lining are suspected.

Q: How can bladder problems be managed?

A: The key to managing bladder problems is understanding the neurologic status of the bladder and the relationship between fluid intake and a full bladder. A three day diary of fluid intake, the time and quantity of urine voided, and episodes of leaking urine is important in establishing a treatment program for bladder problems. Intervention strategies may include timing fluid intake and voiding by the clock rather than waiting for urgency to occur. Protective undergarments can be used if incontinence continues to be a problem. Drugs can be used to decrease the hypersensitivity of the bladder to filling or to relax a spastic sphincter. Intermittent self-catheterization is a strategy that works for many people in both relieving symptoms and preventing potentially serious complications. Sometimes the benefit of an indwelling catheter outweighs the increased risk of infections and stone formation. Surgical interventions are a last resort and rarely indicated.

Q: Are there specific exercises to help manage bladder problems?

A: Muscles in the floor of the pelvis contribute to the ability to store urine in the bladder until it is appropriate to urinate. It is not uncommon for women to have weak muscles in the floor of the pelvis. Kegel exercises, in which these muscles are consciously contracted about two hundred times a day, can strengthen them and decrease the type of incontinence that occurs when bladder pressure exceeds sphincter contraction during coughing or sneezing, for example. Biofeedback is also very helpful in learning how to exercise pelvic floor muscles.

Abdominal muscles help empty the bladder and they can also be strengthened through exercise.

Q: Is autonomic dysreflexia a real threat to patients with MS?

A: Autonomic dysreflexia occurs when there is a complete transection of the spinal cord above the sacral reflex arc. When this occurs the stretched bladder or rectum stimulates the autonomic nervous system and messages from the brain to suppress dangerously elevated blood pressure and other physiologic responses cannot get past the spinal cord injury. It is very rare for someone with MS to have plaques that result in complete functional interruption of the spinal cord.

Q: Is acupuncture helpful for MS bladder problems?

A: There is much about acupuncture that we do not clearly understand. It seems to be very beneficial for some symptoms of MS in some people, particularly pain-related symptoms. There is no evidence that acupuncture alters bladder function in MS in the long term.

Q: What can be done about bowel problems in MS?

A: Normal bowel movements require adequate fluid and fiber in the diet to maintain a soft consistency of stool. The ability to contract and relax the anal sphincter at will is also necessary. A high fiber diet with at least forty-eight ounces of fluid a day and a regular time for having a bowel movement are essential components of a bowel management program. Eating breakfast that includes a warm liquid capitalizes on the natural gastrocolic reflex and encourages bowel emptying at a predictable time. Occasionally it is necessary to add a suppository to a bowel program. The regular use of laxatives is rarely indicated.

Fatigue

Q: Does everyone with MS experience fatigue?

A: Fatigue is the most common symptom in MS. The exact cause of MS fatigue is not known, but it is known that it is related to myelin damage. Muscle weakness can result in increased energy requirements to carry out the common activities of daily living. Pain or stress can also alter sleep patterns, thus producing another type of fatigue from inadequate sleep. The type of fatigue experienced by persons with MS appears to be unique to the disorder and not just an extreme form of the "tiredness" we all feel from time to time.

Q: When symptoms increase in intensity during the day, is it better to continue at the current pace or slack off?

A: A person with MS who has fatigue in the afternoon or after sustained activity should definitely take a period of rest. Rest can improve the ability to function during the remainder of the day.

Q: How can a physiatrist help with fatigue?

A: A physiatrist is a physician who has specialized in rehabilitation. Much of what is involved in the management of MS is rehabilitation. For example, the physiatrist can help prevent contractures and complications, which would result in the need for more energy for the person to carry out activities of daily living. The physiatrist can also prescribe equipment that conserves energy and lessens fatigue.

Q: How can one distinguish between fatigue that is necessary to build stamina and fatigue that could cause an exacerbation of MS?

A: Evidence from recent research indicates that fatigue from exercise will not produce an exacerbation. The negative aspect of fatigue in the person with MS is that in some people—but probably very few—the feeling of tiredness may be prolonged to the point that it makes the benefits of exercise not worth the trade-off. However, muscle fatigue is an essential part of obtaining maximal benefit from exercise. The ideal is to get enough exercise of muscles without excessive tiredness or central fatigue. An individual's prescription for exercise can balance these elements.

Q: Why do symptoms of MS get worse with exercise?

A: They usually don't. However, there is a temperature at which nerve conduction takes place most efficiently. When there is demyelination of nerve fibers in the spinal cord or brain, the sensitivity to elevation in temperature is greater than in unaffected, normally myelinated nerve fibers. Exercise increases core body temperature, which can result in impaired nerve conduction and increases fatigue or temporary worsening of other symptoms.

Q: What strategies can be used to reduce overheating during exercise?

A: Pay attention to the environment. Exercise in a cool room with low humidity or in the shade. Low humidity increases evaporation of perspiration. Eat ice chips while exercising. A commercially available cooling vest can also keep core body temperature from increasing during exercise.

Q: Are there any medications that will reduce fatigue?

A: Amantadine is the drug of choice in treating the fatigue associated with MS. It is a safe medication that can be helpful in about one-third of people with MS. Pemoline, a type of stimulant, may be helpful in people who do not respond to amantadine. 4-aminopyridine (4-AP) can reduce symptoms of MS in general, including fatigue. This drug, however, appears to be most effective in people whose symptoms are exacerbated when they become hot, and it is not yet available in the United States. Several new studies are exploring ways to modify the peripheral as well as central effects of fatigue.

Q: What is the relationship between fatigue and depression in MS?

A: Depression in MS may be "organic" and result from demyelination in the brain. It also may be "reactive" and a consequence of the personal loss brought about by MS. Depression interferes with normal eating and sleeping patterns and generally makes people tired. Antidepressants are an appropriate way to manage the fatigue that results from depression.

Tremor and Spasms

Q: Is there any treatment for tremor?

A: Tremor is a very difficult problem to treat. One treatment that has essentially no side effects is the use of a weight on an extremity to increase its mass, and thus reduce the extent of the tremor. For example, a five-pound weight can be strapped to the wrist to assist in eating or self-care. Several medications also have been reported to help and can be tried, such as propranolol or isoniazid. Our experience with these drugs has generally been disappointing.

Q: What exercises can be done to decrease leg tremor when standing?

A: Shaking of a person's legs may be due to spasticity, ataxia, or muscle weakness. Management depends on which of these problems is causing the symptom. Stretching a tight muscle can help reduce the stretch reflex in a spastic muscle, as well as allowing better joint position. Consequently less muscle energy is required to stand, and leg shaking may be reduced. Pharmacologic treatment is almost always also indicated, with baclofen generally the most effective medication. Too much should be avoided, as that might produce additional weakness. (Small amounts of spasticity may actually enhance standing in weak muscles.) If the problem is ataxia, ankle weights may also reduce shaking, much in the same way that wrist weights can reduce upper limb ataxia.

Q: What can be done about the lumps or bumps in muscle fibers associated with muscle spasms?

A: MS can produce spasms in muscles, but in general the whole muscle becomes tight and reflexes become exaggerated. There is a condition known as myofascial pain or fibrositis that causes muscle pain. This can cause "lumps" in muscles so that they feel like ropes when rubbed or palpated. There is no laboratory test to diagnosis fibrositis. Lumps and bumps in muscles are more likely to be related to fibrositic problems than to MS.

Q: What are the current recommendations for nighttime muscle spasms?

A: Spasms can be related to MS or may be simple muscle cramps identical to those that occur in people without MS. Multiple sclerosis can increase spasticity in muscles, and certain positions in bed can trigger this spasticity. There are two approaches to management. One is to stretch the affected muscle before bedtime so that the stretch reflex of that muscle will not be set off by a small amount of movement. The second is to use a pharmacologic agent such as baclofen to treat spasticity. A combination of stretching exercises, physical therapy, and pharmacologic intervention may be necessary to control nighttime muscle spasms.

Q: What nonpharmacologic strategies can be used to deal with painful spasms?

A: Physical medicine interventions are the best strategies for alleviating painful muscle spasms. Stretching and other exercises can help ameliorate these symptoms. Physicians who specialize in physical medicine and rehabilitation (physiatrists) and physical therapists can assess the problem and prescribe strategies specific to each individual.

Q: What can you tell us about myoclonic jerks?

A: Myoclonic jerks and twitches commonly occur as an individual falls asleep and do not need intervention. If these jerks become a serious problem, drugs used to treat myoclonic epilepsy can be tried. A neurologist or physiatrist can accurately diagnose the problem and prescribe pharmacologic intervention.

Q: What medications are used to treat spasms in MS?

A: Oral baclofen is the initial drug of choice for the pharmacologic treatment of spasticity in MS. Side effects of this medication can be drowsiness and fatigue. Nausea is also possible but can be avoided by taking the medication with food. Some patients, however, benefit from high doses of baclofen but have too many side effects. If spasticity is primarily limited to the lower limbs, a small catheter can be placed in the spinal canal and connected to a small implanted pump that administers baclofen directly to the spinal cord. This form of baclofen administration is very effective for those patients whose spasticity is in the lower limbs and who cannot take oral baclofen. Other drugs that may also be used for spasticity include dantrolene sodium and diazepam. Some patients benefit from a regimen of combination therapy.

Q: Are new anti-inflammatory drugs helpful for muscle spasms?

A: Anti-inflammatory drugs are not effective for muscle spasms. These drugs, which include aspirin, corticosteroids, and nonsteroidal anti-inflammatories (NSAIDs) are used to treat inflammation of tissue such as occurs in arthritis.

Pain

Q: How prevalent is pain with MS?

A: Pain is not an uncommon problem in people with MS. It can result from a variety of problems. Often pain results because muscles become fatigued and stretched when they are used to compensate for muscles that have been weakened by MS. Muscle spasms can also cause pain. People with MS may also experience a kind of pain, called central pain, that results from faulty nerve signals produced by demyelination in the spinal cord or brain. People with MS can develop other painful health conditions as well. Never assume that new pain is "just my MS," but have it evaluated by your health care provider.

Q: What causes musculoskeletal pain?

A: A person with MS is just as vulnerable as anyone else to having pain from muscles, tendons, joints, and bones. A person with MS may actually have a greater tendency for these types of pain because they may not have normal joint range and muscle function.

Q: Aside from musculoskeletal pain, what else causes pain in MS?

A: People with MS also have a "neuritic" type of pain, described as burning, constricting, or tingling. The damaged area of the spinal cord or brain incorrectly interprets pain signals as coming from another part of the body. Sometimes normal touching of skin is interpreted as pain because of mixed-up messages in the central nervous system.

Q: Why is back pain so common in MS?

A: Back pain is a major health care problem in this country. It is the single most common cause of missed work for people without MS. Weakened muscles in the back and abdomen are often a factor in back pain. The best treatment for most cases of acute or chronic back pain is exercise. Unfortunately, people with MS do not always have the ability to generate sufficient intramuscular tension necessary to produce muscular hypertrophy. Therefore, building up the muscles in the back and abdomen may not be an option. Use of a corset during periods of acute back strain can be an effective way to compensate for weakened muscles.

Q: Can specific exercises help to control pain?

A: Pain that results from muscle imbalance can very effectively be decreased by exercise. Each person will require careful evaluation by a knowledgeable health care provider such as a physiatrist or a physical therapist to determine what muscles are weak and which are compensating. An individualized exercise program can be prescribed based on that information. Exercise should also help to decrease spasticity and soreness of those muscles.

Q: What drugs can be used to relieve excruciating pain?

A: The most disturbing pain in MS is that from damage to myelin in the central nervous system. This pain cannot be relieved by usual pain-relieving drugs such as aspirin or narcotics because they do not address the central issue of what is causing the pain. Some drugs used to treat seizures, such as Dilantin®, Depakote®, or Tegretol®, are often effective in treating this central pain, as is a common antidepressant, Elavil®. Non-pharmacologic strategies are often the most effective.

Q: How can chronic pain be managed without drugs?

A: Relaxation techniques such as progressive relaxation, meditation, and deep breathing can contribute to the management of chronic pain. Biofeedback can also be used to learn ways of relaxing muscle groups that are causing pain. Many people have found that massage and chiropractic treatments are helpful in relieving muscle pains. Application of a warm moist cloth to an area that feels as if it is burning may stop the burning sensation for several hours. The application of ice to painful muscles for brief periods of time decreases pain. The transcutaneous electrical nerve stimulator (TENS) may also relieve pain. Hydrotherapy is also useful in relieving some kinds of pain in MS.

Q: If a warm cloth helps relieve tingling, would a heating pad work?

A: There is something about the moist heat for ten to fifteen minutes that really does help. The danger of using a heating pad is that if it goes on too long, there is a much higher danger of burning skin that already has some changes in sensation and may not perceive that the heating pad is becoming too hot.

Q: Can anything be done to minimize skin sensitivity?

A: Skin sensitivity in MS usually results from some damage to the sensory pathways, which makes them over-respond to normal stimuli. Often sensitivity is more pronounced with light touch. Wearing clothing that is very loose is more comfortable than something that fits more snugly. If the problem is disabling, certain drugs used to treat seizures may decrease the sensitivity.

Q: What information is available for MS patients who suffer with headaches.

A: A person with MS can develop every other type of medical problem experienced by anyone else. Someone with headaches should consult a health care practitioner to determine whether these headaches are related to something other than MS. For example, headaches caused by degenerative changes in the cervical spine or migraine problems can occur in people with MS. They are not related to MS and can be effectively treated.

10

Weakness

Q: What is the status of electronic devices to stimulate the limbs?

A: A person with MS has some unique characteristics that may make electrical stimulation techniques more widely used in the future. Specifically, MS lesions are in the central nervous system: the brain and spinal cord. The peripheral nerves, which go from the spinal cord into the muscles in the limbs, are unaffected by MS. Muscles may be weak because the electrical signals cannot get through the central nervous system. Techniques that give messages directly to the peripheral nervous system have the potential for a very good treatment outcome. In some cases electrical stimulation is superior to bracing for weak muscles that cause foot drop.

Q: Can electrical stimulation strengthen muscles?

A: There is some evidence that electrical stimulation combined with voluntary exercise will produce more impressive hypertrophy of muscles in MS than either technique alone. The upper motor neurons are impaired in MS and electrical stimulation can, in a sense, substitute for a person's own activation of the brain and spinal cord to provide stimulation for peripheral nerves.

Memory Difficulties and
Other Cognitive Problems

Q: How many people with MS have memory loss?

A: No one knows exactly how many people actually have MS, let alone how many of those people have which symptoms. Memory problems are certainly a major concern for many people with MS. Some studies have estimated that as few as 10 percent or as many as 90 percent of people with MS have some degree of memory impairment, usually in what is referred to as "short-term" memory. The majority of people with cognitive dysfunction continue to function without significant difficulty.

Q: What kind of memory is affected by MS?

A: There are two aspects of memory. One is the ability to remember things immediately—the type of memory necessary to acquire new information. The second component of memory is the ability to retrieve stored information. It has been assumed that people with MS had difficulty retrieving information, but newer information suggests that they may also have problems acquiring information. The parts of memory that are affected by the disease are being studied, but it will be a few years before good data are available.

Q: What causes memory loss in someone with MS?

A: Sometimes memory problems are a result of actual structural damage from demyelination within the brain. At other times memory impairment is related to other problems such as the side effects of drugs or the effects of stress. Sometimes MS is used as an excuse for being unable to remember things that someone without the disease cannot remember either! Short-term memory impairment is often a result of not paying attention to the content in the first place. (Teenagers and spouses often experience this type of memory impairment!)

Q: Is there an exercise or special diet or vitamin that improves memory?

A: Although fish has been claimed to be "brain food," there is no evidence that fish or any other food or dietary supplement improves memory. However, there are strategies to help improve memory, such as using associations to learn new material. Libraries and bookstores have many self-help guides to improving memory.

Q: Do plasma infusions help memory loss and poor concentration?

A: Plasma infusions or plasmapheresis do not help memory loss or poor concentration caused by destruction of myelin in the central nervous system. However, memory problems also may be caused by the side effects of medications used to treat spasticity, pain, or other symptoms in MS, so this possibility should also be explored.

Q: Are there cognitive skills besides memory that may be impaired with MS?

A: Cognitive skills include attention, learning, memory, language, and thought. Demyelination of areas of the brain that control these functions can cause problems in any of these areas. It is not a wise idea to attribute problems with remembering, planning, thinking ahead, or judgment to demyelination without investigation. These problems often result from the side effects of drugs, stress, or even other diseases such as vascular disease, diabetes, lung or heart disease, or nutritional deficiencies. Neuropsychological testing may be suggested as one means to help analyze the difficulty.

Communication Disorders:
Hearing, Speech, and Vision

Q: Is hearing loss normal with MS?

A: Multiple sclerosis can cause inflammation, blocks of nerve conduction, and demyelination in many parts of the central nervous system (CNS), including the brain stem, the area where the acoustic nerve arises. When this occurs, the resultant ringing in the ears and loss of hearing can be difficult to treat. Intravenous (IV) corticosteroids such as methylprednisolone may help during an acute exacerbation, but they will not help a chronic problem.

Q: Can speech therapy help someone with MS whose speech is affected?

A: The most common cause of speech problems in MS is due to an impairment in the muscles needed for speaking. Speech may become slurred and difficult to understand. Speech therapists have a variety of techniques that may improve communication, even though the problem cannot be cured. Another problem arises when chest muscles are weak and the person's speaking is soft because he cannot get enough air behind his voice. Personal amplifier systems are inexpensive and work well to overcome this problem.

Q: What vision problems can affect people with MS?

A: Multiple sclerosis may effect the optic nerve (actually an extension of the CNS) to the eye, which results in some impairment in vision. People often describe this as having "blind spots" or "like looking through a lace curtain." Currently, the most effective treatment for damage to the optic nerve is intravenous corticosteroids used for an acute exacerbation. Fortunately, however, visual problems of this type are usually self-limited and may improve in time. Some people have double vision because of eye muscle weakness. Unfortunately, double vision in MS is usually dynamic—it changes too rapidly for a prism in eyeglasses to be effective. Wearing a patch over one eye stops double vision. It is important to change the eye patch from one eye to the other on a regular basis or the patched eye will develop reduced vision.

Q: What communication aids are available when a person is unable to speak and has limited use of her hands and head.

A: The technology in nonvocal communication is improving constantly. There are a variety of communicators that actually speak or display a printed message based on the individual's ability to spell out words or to recognize words on a board. Those communication systems can interface with very simple on-off switches. Consultation with a speech pathologist and a bioengineer can often solve communication problems.

Q: Do insurance companies pay for communicators?

A: Often insurance companies do not cover communication devices. There is incredible pressure from society to reduce the amount of money spent on health care. Technology is advancing, but it is very expensive. Health care reform is likely to have an adverse effect on the provision of sophisticated technology to help disabled people. It is important to contact policymakers in the House of Representatives and the Senate, on both the national and the state levels, as well as policymakers in insurance companies, to remind them not to leave the needs of disabled people out of the health care system.

Effect of Temperature on Symptoms

Q: Can heat make MS worse?

A: In the long term, heat probably does not make MS worse. However, when the core body temperature is raised, fatigue and other symptoms of MS become more apparent in most, but not all, people with MS. This is a short-term effect, and symptoms abate when core body temperature returns to normal. Nerve impulses are transmitted best at normal body temperature. A rise in core body temperature impairs nerve conduction in demyelinated nerves. The combined effect of damaged myelin and heat contribute to the worsening of symptoms. For those people who are sensitive to heat, it is important to stay in a cool environment with low humidity.

Q: How can core body temperature be kept down?

A: Stay in a cool environment with low humidity. However, that is easier said than done in many climates. A cool environment can be achieved through air conditioning. If the home is not air conditioned, this is a legitimate income tax deduction as a medical expense. Spend time in shopping centers, movie theaters, or other buildings that have air conditioning. Stay in the shade rather than in the direct sun.

Q: When a cool environment is not possible, what else can be done?

A: Some simple things can help someone with MS to stay cool. Eat ice chips or drink cold beverages. A cold wet washcloth on the back of the neck helps cooling. Swim in cool water or wear a cooling vest. There are two types of cooling vests available. One has pockets in which you insert blue ice, while the other contains coils that carry a coolant connected to a small refrigeration unit.

Q: Why is low humidity important in maintaining core body temperature?

A: Normally when core body temperature rises, the body turns on its own "air conditioning system," and air evaporates perspiration to produce a cooling effect. Lightweight clothing made of fabric that wicks perspiration away from the body aids in evaporation. More fluid intake is required in hot humid weather because the body is excreting more water through perspiration.

Q: How can you avoid overheating while exercising?

A: The key is to be able to exercise to maximum capacity yet produce a minimal increase in core body temperature. Exercise in a low humidity, cool environment so that the cooling mechanisms of the body can take effect. Follow the suggestions above for staying cool. Symptoms brought on by or exacerbated by heat associated with exercise will disappear when core body temperature returns to normal.

Q: What is the effect of temperature on emotional attitudes?

A: Impaired nerve conduction caused by elevated core body temperature can affect what are called "higher functions," such as memory, problem solving, and emotions, just as it can affect the function of arms or legs. Heat does not change the psychological make-up of a person with MS, but it can make people depressed and angry about the effect the disease is having on their life. A health care professional skilled in assessing and managing psychological problems, such as a psychologist or psychologic social worker, can determine the etiology of behavior changes and the best treatment possible.

Q: Is everyone with MS sensitive to heat?

A: Heat sensitivity is common but not universal in MS. Many people without the disease do not like the heat, but MS heat sensitivity is unique to people with MS. Just like people without MS, some people are hot most of the time and others are cold most of the time. Cold feet can occur as a result of impaired circulation when a person does not have sufficient muscle tone in her/his legs to assist blood circulation. If this is a problem, wearing wool socks or a double layer of socks is a safe way to keep feet warm.

Q: What is the effect of cold on MS?

A: Certain symptoms of MS seem to be more pronounced in cold temperatures. Swimming in cold water may make muscle spasms worse. Cool weather seems to be less a problem than hot weather because it is often easier to keep warm by layering clothing. Also, cool weather does not induce the "heat sensitivity" so typical of some people with MS.

Multiple Sclerosis and Other Medical Conditions

Q: How does MS affect allergies?

A: Multiple sclerosis appears to be an autoimmune disease. The immune system is incredibly complex, and anything that affects the immune system has implications for MS. Certainly allergies, other infections, and other autoimmune diseases need to be kept in mind when the immune system is not functioning ideally.

Q: What is the connection between silicon breast implants and MS?

A: Ruptured silicon breast implants have been reported to cause symptoms that somewhat resemble MS. Silicon does not cause MS but may cause similar symptoms. The mechanism of silicon disease is not understood.

Q: What is the relationship between MS and insulin-dependent diabetes?

A: Insulin-dependent diabetes and multiple sclerosis are two totally separate disorders although both are believed to be autoimmune disorders. Corticosteroids have been used extensively to treat MS. One of the side effects of corticosteroids is that they can actually produce a diabetic state that requires insulin.

Q: What can be done to manage vagus nerve damage from MS that affects the heart?

A: The heart has its own built-in regulation and pacemaker, unlike skeletal muscle which requires nerve signals from the brain and spinal cord to function. MS can affect parts of the brain and spinal cord that control organs such as the lungs and possibly the heart. MS does not affect peripheral nerves like the vagus nerve per se. Rarely MS might affect some of the nuclei in the brain stem that control and are related to function of the vagus nerve.

Q: Is there evidence that smoking has a specific detrimental effect on MS?

A: Smoking has very detrimental effects on health in general. There is no specific evidence that smoking is any worse for people with MS than it is for the general population. Smoking causes lung disease, which impairs breathing. This may be compounded by chest muscle weakness in MS. Cigarette smoke adversely affects blood vessels, which may contribute to impaired peripheral circulation, coronary artery disease, and stroke. In no way is smoking good for anyone, with or without MS.

Q: Should people with MS get the flu vaccine?

A: People with MS should get the influenza vaccine, especially if they have some involvement of chest muscles that would put them at risk for developing pneumonia. Over a decade ago some people who received the flu vaccine developed an acute neurologic disease called Guillian-Barré syndrome. Investigation of that incident found a defective batch of the vaccine. Although some older books caution against it, we believe that there is no convincing current evidence that the vaccine exacerbates MS or causes other serious problems.

Q: Why does it take so long to get over the flu or a cold?

A: These illnesses often produce fever. When the core body temperature is increased, conduction in the demyelinated segments of the central nervous system is altered and conduction blocks that impair neurologic function can develop. When this occurs, the normal healthy status of the person is impaired. Some functional ability may be lost during that time which may take a while to regain. Some persons with MS may also have weakened respiratory muscles. It should not take longer to get rid of an infection just because you have MS. However, your body's ability to "bounce back" may be slower.

Q: Why does an exacerbation often follow a bout of flu?

A: Influenza, a viral infection, stresses the body and calls on the immune system to rid the body of the virus. The additional demands on the body's immune system can predispose the person to a worsening of MS symptoms. Fever is commonly associated with influenza. As normal nerve conduction in the central nervous system is slowed by the increase in body temperature, impulses across demyelinated nerve may become significantly impaired, causing symptoms that are not apparent at normal body temperature.

Q: Does MS protect you from getting other diseases?

A: It would be nice to think that MS brought with it some immunity to other major illnesses but, in fact, that is not true. People with MS can get cancer, they can have heart attacks, they can get acute illnesses like the flu and so forth. Maintaining your general health and participating in programs that decrease your risk factors for those other health problems is just as important for people with MS as it is for others. A low fat diet, giving up smoking, and exercising are some lifestyle modifications that markedly decrease risk for heart disease and strokes. Be sure that you regularly have the recommended screening to detect other serious medical problems early.

Q: Have any studies been done on the relationship between MS and ADHD?

A: To our knowledge, there has not been any research directly linking attention deficit hyperactivity disorder (ADHD) to multiple sclerosis.

15

Surgery and Its Effects on MS

Q: What advice do you have for people who need to have surgery and will be receiving anesthesia?

A: Surgery is a major stressor on the body, and it is speculated that this level of stress can result in an exacerbation in some MS patients. The stress may produce an immediate exacerbation, one that is somewhat delayed, or have no impact. The evidence is not conclusive. If surgery is necessary, be sure that your general health is as good as it can be before you go through surgery.

Q: Will immobilization of an extremity following surgery adversely affect MS?

A: Immobilization of a limb following a major surgical procedure such as a tendon repair may result in muscle atrophy and contracture of joints. The ability to bounce back from a period of immobilization is diminished in someone with MS. Electrical stimulation of nerves and muscles during the period the limb is immobilized might be helpful, and special rehabilitative efforts following surgery should be implemented.

III

WELLNESS MANAGEMENT

There are very few sources of information available on topics covered in this section for people with MS. In this section, we answer questions that relate to empowerment of people with MS to take control of their lives and maintain wellness. People who take charge of their lives and take responsibility for their behavior do far better than those who assume a passive stance. People with MS need to make a determination that they care about their health and make it their highest priority.

Exercises are important to maintaining wellness. They are not only a scientifically valid means of increasing strength in people with weakness and a means of stretching tight muscles and preserving range of motion of contracted joints, but they also help give a sense of well-being to the person who exercises. Conclusions from recent studies on exercise and MS have shown that exercises of various types—stretching/range of motion, resistive/strength building, and aerobic/cardiovascular all have important roles in the management of MS.

At one time, when very little could be done for people with MS, dietary management was held in high esteem as a therapeutic intervention by some physicians and many patients. Scientific evidence has not supported the usefulness of any particular diet for MS. However, healthful eating is essential. People with MS are not immune to the number one killer in our country—cardiovascular disease. The American Heart Association suggests that not more than 25–30% of our diet come from fat. Sound nutritional principles include eating more complex carbohydrates, fruits, vegetables, and whole grains. People who eat right feel better—and that's not just emotional, it's physiological.

Exercise

Q: Is there a particular type of exercise that is best for people with MS?

A: The type of exercise that is best for someone with MS depends on the severity and extent of the disease process, as well as on age and other health characteristics. For example, a young, newly diagnosed person with MS who is otherwise healthy may have essentially no limitations on physical activity and would benefit from the same types of exercise as anyone without MS. In a more severe situation, in which MS has progressed and weakness is a problem, the best type of exercises might be range of motion, in which the joints are taken through full range and the muscles are stretched, possibly along with specific resistive exercises for certain weakened muscles. Of course, concomitant diseases such as arthritis might produce other restrictions on physical activity.

Q: Is aerobic exercise beneficial to someone with MS?

A: Aerobic exercises are conditioning exercises for the cardiovascular system. A person with MS who has the physical capacity to participate in an aerobic exercise program will certainly benefit. However, some people may be limited by fatigue. Aerobic exercise will not alter the course of MS, but it may improve general health.

Q: How much research has been done on exercise and MS?

A: The National Multiple Sclerosis Society has funded some studies on exercise and multiple sclerosis. We know that exercise in someone without MS builds strength. It also increases core body temperature, which may temporarily worsen some symptoms of MS in certain susceptible people. However, it appears to be helpful for many people with MS.

Q: Are weight bearing exercises that do not raise core body temperature helpful?

A: Weight bearing exercises have a positive effect on bone metabolism. Standing in parallel bars can decrease osteoporosis and improve heart, lung, and kidney function. It is also good psychologically to be able to stand up and face people at eye level. One disadvantage of exercising in water is that the buoyancy of the water does not provide the benefit of weight bearing, although hydrotherapy can be excellent for maintaining joint range of motion.

Q: Can too much exercise bring on an exacerbation of MS?

A: No. Exercise does not appear to precipitate an exacerbation of MS. However, exercise that raises core body temperature may temporarily worsen symptoms. This worsening of symptoms will resolve reasonably soon after the activity is stopped and body temperature returns to normal.

Q: Are there specific exercises that will strengthen leg muscles?

A: Exercise that involves lifting a weight or pushing against resistance can produce muscular fatigue. In fact, in healthy subjects the most effective way to strengthen a muscle is to exercise it to the point of fatigue. The problem in someone with MS is that another type of fatigue—central fatigue—can occur and possibly interfere with the strengthening "muscle fatigue." Also, the level of force that can be generated in weak muscles in people with MS is reduced, so exercise may not be efficient. It is not uncommon, for example, for someone with MS to be able to walk a short distance without difficulty. However, walking a long distance may result in foot drop. It is important for the person with MS to get an expert opinion as to whether exercise, the adjustment of medicine to reduce spasticity, or the use of ambulation aids and ankle foot orthoses (braces) to protect muscles that fatigue easily is indicated.

Q: Can someone with MS go beyond physical limits daily or periodically without harm?

A: Many people with MS will have some physical limitations. Certain levels of activities will be comfortable, beyond which there will be a feeling of exhaustion. There is no harm at times, in pushing those limits into the range of exhaustion. However, persistent exhaustion and fatigue can be detrimental.

Q: What is the optimum exercise for people who are barely ambulatory?

A: Range of motion exercises are the first recommendation. Moving the joints through their *full* range of motion only once a day prevents the development of contractures that interfere with joint movement and impair the ability to perform activities of daily living. Any resistive exercise, that is, moving a limb against a resistance or weight, might help or hinder. A physiatrist or physical therapist can determine the most appropriate exercises.

Q: How does someone with MS know when he or she has enough exercise?

A: Someone with MS needs enough exercise to maintain cardiovascular fitness and muscular strength, but not so much exercise as to become exhausted. That particular point is very individualized. Working with a physiatrist, physical therapist, or exercise physiologist can help each individual determine an exercise level that is appropriate to his current level of ability.

Q: What kind of exercises are appropriate for someone with numbness and tingling?

A: Exercises are really not used for treatment of numbness and tingling that result from damage to myelin in the central nervous system. Numbness and tingling can also result from peripheral nerve compression or impaired blood circulation. Specific exercises might help to alleviate numbness and tingling from these causes.

Q: Can someone in a wheelchair participate in aerobic exercise?

A: Much will depend on why the person is in a wheelchair and how much muscle function remains in the legs. Upper body exercises can be done even when it is not possible to exercise the lower body, but they are less efficient in providing aerobic conditioning than are the large muscles of the lower limbs. There are videotapes and other exercise resources that demonstrate exercise programs for people with varying abilities (see Appendix A). Consultation with a physiatrist, physical therapist, or exercise physiologist can result in an individual program that will help increase cardiovascular fitness, even though a person may be seriously disabled.

Q: Can strenuous exercise hurt someone with MS?

A: Strenuous exercise in someone with MS should not cause harm. The question to be asked is how long the degree of fatigue that results from the exercise lasts. If the fatigue from strenuous exercise continues into the next day, cutting back on the exercise would be appropriate. Otherwise, it is good to continue exercise at the maximum level possible. A good rule of thumb is that it should not take much longer to recover from exercise than it took to become fatigued.

Q: Is it possible for someone with MS to cross the line of too much exercise?

A: It is possible for someone who has fairly advanced MS and who is very motivated and driven to cross the line into an area where they are losing more than they are gaining from exercise. For example, theoretically, lifting weights with muscles that cannot achieve the degree of tension within the muscle required to increase muscle strength and produce muscle fiber hypertrophy may simply cause fatigue without beneficial effects. Yet, there is recent evidence that some improvement in strength and function may occur, even in these muscles. Exercise tolerance may change over the course of MS and the individual's exercise program should be modified accordingly from time to time.

Q: Is it best to exercise every day on a certain schedule?

A: Consistent exercise is required to obtain beneficial effects. Ideally, aerobic exercises should be done for at least twenty minutes three times a week. The time of day that someone exercises should correspond with the times when they have most energy. Normal body temperature tends to be lowest in the morning and gradually rises to a peak in late afternoon. Exercising in the morning when body temperature is lowest helps to prevent heat-induced fatigue.

Q: Should someone who develops tingling or shaking in their legs continue to exercise?

A: Tingling that occurs only with exercise could be a sign of elevated core body temperature or another problem such as nerve compression or peripheral vascular disease. Evaluation by a health care professional can help to sort out the cause of new symptoms during exercise and let you know if you should modify the exercise.

Q: What should a person do who cannot move his or her legs or arms?

A: Exercise is much more than just lifting weights. Exercise includes such things as passive exercises where a therapist or family member takes a joint through a full range of motion. This can be done even though a person has essentially no strength in that limb. Without normal movement muscles and tendons can shorten, causing contractures, and ligaments around joints can stiffen, tightening joints. Contractures and frozen joints can result in serious skin breakdown. Therefore, some type of "exercise" is desirable for all people with MS.

Q: Is an exercise tolerance test on a treadmill necessary before engaging in aerobic exercise?

A: The purpose of a treadmill test is to determine the optimal and safe level of exercise prior to engaging in a vigorous program. Some people who have not exercised as they have gotten older can experience ischemic changes in the heart with exercise. The treadmill uses an electrocardiogram to monitor changes in the heart with progressive exercise. A treadmill test is a good idea for anyone over forty years of age who has not been exercising and who plans to start an extremely vigorous exercise program, or for anyone with an indication of a heart problem.

Q: Can someone with MS improve strength through exercise?

A: In order to increase strength in a muscle, certain characteristics of contraction must occur within the muscle fibers. Ideally, for the most efficient increase in strength, contractions must approach two-thirds of the maximal isometric tension within a muscle and be sustained for a brief period of time. That is a pretty stiff order for someone who has MS. To whatever extent an exercise falls short of that level of intensity, the degree of muscle hypertrophy that results will be less marked. Some increase in strength will occur, but it will take longer to achieve. Demyelination interferes with messages from the brain to the muscles telling them to contract, so muscle exercises and muscle building will be suboptimal. That should not be used as an excuse to abandon exercise, however.

Q: What should a person do when muscles cramp during exercise?

A: Any exercise that makes symptoms worse or brings on other symptoms is probably inappropriate or is being done incorrectly. Gentle, slow stretching of a muscle before doing the exercise is usually helpful in preventing cramps.

Q: What is the relationship between exercise and blood pressure?

A: With exercise there is a short-term, transient increase in blood pressure. In the long run, a healthy person should have a sustained drop in blood pressure as a result of exercise. Weight loss, exercise, and sodium restriction are the major nonpharmacologic strategies for dealing with high blood pressure.

Q: Should a stiff joint be forced during exercise?

A: A stiff joint may be caused by a contracture of the soft tissue surrounding the joint. Sudden forcing of the joint beyond its normal range can be harmful and can cause damage to the soft tissue in the capsule around the joint. A safer and more effective therapy is a static stretch, in which a low force is applied to the joint for a period of about five to twenty minutes to gently force the joint beyond its contracted range. The application of heat can also help to get a better result from the stretch.

Swimming

Q: Is swimming good for people with MS?

A: Swimming and water aerobics are very popular among the MS community, probably because they allow a person who is weak or has some ataxia to be able to use the buoyancy of water in order to perform activities they could not do otherwise. Swimming and water aerobics are also strength-building exercises because moving through water produces a mild resistance, and resistance helps increase strength. A person with ataxia may be able to do things in the water that are not possible otherwise because the resistance of the water decreases the uncoordinated movements somewhat.

Q: Can swimming get your heart rate into the target range and assist with weight loss?

A: Certainly long distance swimming can increase your heart rate to within target range. Swimming laps in an Olympic pool or water aerobics that burn calories in excess of calories taken in food will assist with weight loss. However, it would take a great deal of swimming to make a significant difference in weight. Swimming tones muscles, which contributes to the visual effect of a fit body.

Q: What is the appropriate temperature of a pool for someone with MS?

A: Typically pool temperatures between 85° and 88° Fahrenheit appear to be good for people with MS. Temperatures as high as 92° may feel good and are excellent for people with arthritis, but that temperature may increase fatigue and other symptoms of MS. Water temperature that is too low may precipitate muscle spasms and cramps.

Diet

Q: Do nutritional needs differ among MS patients?

A: There are different dietary requirements for different people. However, the basic vitamins and minerals required each day are the same for everyone within certain age groups. The number of calories needed varies from one individual to another and is unrelated to MS. Someone who has a small frame and a sedentary job needs fewer calories than someone who has a large frame and a large muscle mass and does heavy physical labor. There is no evidence that people with MS need specific dietary modifications.

Q: What type of diet is good for MS?

A: Many diets have been suggested for MS. There is absolutely no scientific evidence that any diet modification alters the course of MS. Good nutrition is a very important aspect of keeping your body in the best possible condition, and the new U.S. government food pyramid is an excellent guide for the daily intake of various nutrients (see Appendix B).

Q: Can a low fat diet help people with MS?

A: Low fat diets have received a great deal of press in recent years. We know much about the adverse effects of a high fat diet on blood vessels and its role in heart attacks, strokes, and certain types of cancer. A low fat diet is not expected to alter the course of MS, but it is a healthy diet that may prevent other serious illnesses.

Q: Are there any controlled studies of diets in MS?

A: Diets are difficult and expensive to study because it is hard for most people to rigidly adhere to a diet. There is much anecdotal information available about people feeling better or noticing a change in symptoms with various dietary modifications. However, there are no rigidly controlled, double blind studies of diets for MS.

Q: Can you recommend a diet that will give high energy and still help to lose weight?

A: Issues of weight loss are an ongoing problem, particularly for people who have a decreased ability to participate in activities that burn calories. Complex carbohydrates, found on the bottom level of the food pyramid (Appendix B), are used by athletes to sustain activity during marathon running and long distance cycling. The portion sizes referred to on the food pyramid are quite small. For example one-half cup of most breakfast cereals constitutes a serving. A full and complete diet, but one that is low in calories, is probably the best.

Q: Can a diet take off inches as well as pounds?

A: Generally speaking, exercise plus diet is more effective than diet alone for taking off inches. Often a person who spends a lot of time sitting in a wheelchair finds that the waistline increases in size. This may be due to weakness of trunk muscles as well as to an increase in fat. Muscle weakness in MS can alter the type of exercise that someone can do. The best approach would be to meet with a physiatrist, a physical therapist, or an exercise physiologist who can evaluate strengths and weaknesses and design an individualized program that will maintain some level of exercise.

Q: What is the best way to lose weight?

A: Sustained weight loss is a long-term project. Crash diets may result in short-term weight loss, but dietary patterns do not change and weight is regained when the diet ends. Severe dietary restriction can result in poor nutrition and increased symptoms of weakness. Balancing food intake with calorie expenditure in a way that does not lead to feelings of deprivation is the only long-term solution to treating the overweight condition. A nutritionist can help plan a diet that includes favorite foods, but is also low in calories and high in vitamins, minerals, and energy.

Q: Does it take longer for the body to digest red meat, and does it contribute to MS fatigue?

A: Eating red meat is related more to the fat content of the meat than to the digestive issue. After a heavy meal all of us find that we are a bit more fatigued because our body's energy is being used to digest food. One way to overcome this problem is to eat lighter, smaller, and more frequent meals. Some people report that they do not feel well after eating red meat, but this is not specifically related to MS.

Q: Is there a connection between the ingestion of dairy products and worsening of symptoms of MS?

A: There is no evidence that dairy products have an adverse effect on MS. Many dairy products are high in fat, and fat is a health hazard. The use of nonfat milk and low fat cheese is a good idea. Some people lack the enzyme to digest lactose in milk products, but that is not related to MS. The symptoms of lactose intolerance are stomach cramps or diarrhea after eating products that contain milk. Lactase enzyme tablets can help this problem.

Q: Have specific foods been implicated in worsening symptoms of MS?

A: Surely someone has reported that foods ranging from potatoes to pork have worsened their symptoms! Although there are many anecdotal stories about the relationship between food and MS, there is absolutely no scientific evidence to support these connections.

Q: What is the effect of caffeine on MS?

A: Caffeine is a stimulant to the nervous system. Some people find they cannot start their morning without caffeine. Caffeinated drinks often get people through the afternoon slump periods. Consequently, caffeine can be useful in helping to manage the symptoms of MS fatigue.

Q: Is sugar beneficial to someone with MS?

A: Fatigue that results from demyelination of nerves is probably not going to be helped by sugar. However, if there is a component of low blood sugar contributing to fatigue, a candy bar may give that extra push. Eating a piece of fruit is a much better choice than eating a candy bar.

Q: Why do steroids cause weight gain?

A: Two things may cause weight gain in a person taking steroids. Steroids affect the sodium and potassium balance in the body. Sodium is retained and keeps water with it so some of the initial weight gain is due to fluid accumulation. This weight disappears rapidly when the drug is discontinued. On a long-term basis, steroids affect metabolism and may result in fat deposits in the trunk of the body.

Q: Can bananas help muscle cramps?

A: Muscle cramps in MS are unlikely to be caused by an imbalance of chemicals in the body. However, bananas and raisins are an excellent source of potassium and are often recommended for people who are taking diuretics that deplete the body of potassium, which may result in cramps.

Q: Do vitamins and other nutritional supplements improve the well-being of a person with MS?

A: There is no evidence that vitamin therapy alters the course of MS or improves well-being. We do know, however, that malnutrition can have adverse effects on nerve and other tissues in the body. It is important for everyone to have a healthful diet full of necessary and appropriate vitamins and minerals. Eating the recommended portions of foods on the U.S. government recommended food pyramid is an excellent way to ensure that nutritional requirements are met.

Q: What is the relationship between MS and vitamin B12?

A: Vitamin B12 is not deficient in MS. People who have an abnormality in gastric secretions such that they are not producing the intrinsic factor necessary for their body to absorb B12 have a disease called pernicious anemia. Pernicious anemia can cause neurologic symptoms that may mimic MS and can be alleviated by vitamin B12 injections or the new sublingual drops. However, MS is not benefited by vitamin B12 injections. Overuse of drugs that block the secretion of stomach acid can result in vitamin B12 deficiencies.

Q: How do herbal remedies help people with MS?

A: No known herb has been shown to alter the course of MS or to replace damaged myelin. However, a variety of herbal preparations have been suggested for management of MS symptoms. Some are a close analog to pharmacologic agents and have similar side effects. The use of herbal medicine requires a knowledge of the herb's intended effects, its side effects, and its long-term effects. Often it takes a lot of reading and talking to experts to get the necessary information about herbal remedies with special attention to potential harmful effects.

Q: Is there any evidence that vitamin supplements affect MS?

A: With certain exceptions, vitamin supplements are not generally recommended for anyone who is eating a well-balanced diet. Vitamins in pills may be metabolized differently than vitamins from natural food sources. Excessive intake of some vitamins, particularly the fat soluble vitamins, can cause major problems because they are not excreted as readily through urine as are the water soluble vitamins. There have been reports that large doses of vitamin B6 can cause neurologic symptoms that can be confused with MS. A generic one-a-day multivitamin can provide insurance that all essential vitamins have been taken for people whose diet is not optimal. Additionally, people might want to consider a supplement of antioxidants—vitamins C, E, and beta carotene—but even these are controversial.

Q: Have fish oils been shown to slow the progression of MS?

A: No. Fish oil is one of the many food substances that has been claimed to help MS in one way or another. Many people have testified that those things help them, but no studies have demonstrated any real effect on MS.

Q: Should someone with MS take antioxidants?

A: Antioxidants may prevent the occurrence of certain forms of cancer. The best way to get adequate supplies of vitamins C and E and beta carotene is through food. There is less evidence that taking them as dietary supplements is as effective, and there is some evidence that they may be harmful. There is no evidence of benefit in MS.

IV

EMOTIONAL HEALTH

The mind and body are integrally connected. Symptoms of MS can make dramatic changes in one's lifestyle. Coping with these stresses challenges the person with MS and his family members. It is often hard to remember that you are still the person you were before MS. Certain personality characteristics help one cope with MS. These characteristics include a desire to work at problems, resilience, and a belief in one's self. Developing effective ways to cope with stress is essential. Another important contribution to maintaining emotional health is to become a key player in your own health care by taking responsibility for your own life and your own body. Approaching the life changes that occur because of MS requires creativity. Creativity involves challenging assumptions, recognizing patterns, seeing things in new ways, making connections, taking risks, taking advantage of chance, and constructing networks.

Stress

Q: What is the effect of stress on the body?

A: There have been many studies on the mind-body connection. Emotions and emotional health have an important effect on physical health. There is a close connection between the immune system and the neurochemicals that are produced in our bodies in response to stressful events. Ongoing stress places the body in a constant state of a fight or flight reaction that can have an adverse effect on the human body.

Q: Should a person with MS avoid stress?

A: Each person responds to stress differently, and different things are stressful for different people. Sometimes even things that are stressful at one time are not stressful at others. High levels of stress are not good for the human body. On the other hand, we cannot live in a totally stress-free environment. Researchers who isolated people and removed all stress from their lives found that without some stress people began to experience hallucinations and other signs of psychosis. Probably the best strategy is to learn to effectively cope with stressors.

Q: Is there a relationship between stress and MS?

A: Certain responses to stress are not good for the human body, whether the person has MS or not. Stress has been known to cause increased symptoms in people with MS. There may be no increase in symptoms during the time of stress, but an exacerbation may occur later, when the body's response has gone back to a more normal level and the production of stress hormones has returned to normal. Several retrospective studies of people with MS have suggested an increase in exacerbations as a delayed response to stress. Retrospective studies can be misleading because subjects may have selective recall of past events.

Q: What are some constructive ways of managing stress?

A: The first thing is to recognize what things are stressful. Different things can be stressful to different people. Most important is to recognize how you respond to stress. Do you feel anger or sadness? Are your palms sweating and heart beating fast? It is essential to know yourself and what works for you. For some people meditation works very well but for others sitting down to meditate will increase their stress level. Exercise in the form of walking or working out works best for some people. Progressive relaxation exercises, guided imagery, or biofeedback can be used to learn relaxation that can be implemented during stressful situations. It is a good idea to sit down with a health care professional and talk about how you respond to stress, what kinds of things are important, and what things you like to do. With this information a program of stress management can be developed that will help to manage stress appropriately.

Q: Does the diagnosis of MS cause mental stress?

A: For many people the diagnosis of MS itself can cause stress. Uncertainty during the diagnostic process is often stressful because there are unfamiliar tests that take a considerable amount of time. Many newly diagnosed people have never heard of MS and do not know what to expect. The diagnosis of MS can reduce stress because it explains the symptoms a person is experiencing.

Coping

Q: What are the relationships between physical, emotional, and spiritual health?

A: Our bodies function as a whole unit; each part of our body affects the function of others. If we are under a great deal of stress and not coping with that stress very well, chemicals are produced in the body that cause sweaty palms, rapid heart beat, increased urine production, and diarrhea. When someone is managing a long-term illness such as MS, it is important to address all parts of their human being, not just the physical symptoms.

Q: What can be expected of medical practitioners in helping someone cope with MS?

A: Many medical specialists have a role in helping to manage MS. A physician—often a neurologist—diagnoses the disease and manages its exacerbations and progression. A physiatrist who is skilled in rehabilitation medicine can help with maintaining optimal function and activities of daily living. A primary health care provider will be concerned about general health, not just MS. Psychologists help people work through coping issues. Social workers can counsel families. Multiple sclerosis and its effect on individuals and family members is complex. No one health care provider can be expected to meet all of the person's needs all the time.

Q: How can people with MS maintain a positive attitude when every exacerbation causes a more painful emotional crisis?

A: Maintaining a positive outlook on life is difficult when you have a disease that continually exacerbates and compromises your ability to maintain independence. One approach is to recognize deficits and focus on the positive. Someone who can no longer run can give up by saying, "Now that I cannot run I will not be able to maintain my physical fitness." Another approach is to say, "I cannot run anymore. How can I get around this? Can I walk? Can I do upper body exercises?"

Q: What role does a positive attitude play in someone with MS?

A: There is a close relationship between our physical well-being and emotional well-being. Anything that maintains emotional well-being will have a positive effect on the body. Symptoms of MS will not be compounded if the body is in good physical shape. Keeping a positive attitude is one strategy for maintaining emotional health, but that must be balanced without denying what is really going on. It is important to use effective strategies for coping with symptoms of MS and not just saying, "I am going to think positively and everything will be fine." Having a support system or other people with whom you can talk about what is going on can go a long way toward cultivating a positive attitude.

Q: How can people with MS cope with the psychological stress that comes from others not understanding their plight?

A: One of the problems that occurs with MS is the "but you look so well" syndrome. Symptoms of MS are often invisible to other people. It is difficult to communicate the real effect that MS has on daily life. Someone cannot just look at you and see that you are fatigued or that you have pain. The National Multiple Sclerosis Society has an ongoing program of public awareness about MS. It is everyone's responsibility to help with that campaign. If each person with multiple sclerosis told five other people what it is really like to have MS, the awareness of MS and its effects would be markedly increased. Only when people begin to understand the diversity and mysteries of living with MS will they begin to respond appropriately to people with the disease.

Mental Health

Q: What is the effect of depression on MS?

A: There are organic as well as nonorganic causes of depression. Depression and fatigue are sometimes difficult to separate. It is important for someone who has problems with depression to consult a health care professional who is familiar with these issues, especially as they relate to MS. It is important to determine how much of the depression is related to organic changes in the brain and how much is a response to stress. Understanding the cause of depression determines whether the depression is treated with antidepressants, with cognitive or behavioral strategies, or, typically, with a combination of both.

Q: Does severe depression coincide with MS demyelination sites?

A: It does appear that some of the depression and psychological problems that occur are related to organic changes in the brain. The National Multiple Sclerosis Society is funding research related to these issues.

Q: Is there any correlation between mood swings and MS?

A: Mood swings are part of human nature. Some people with MS experience mood swings that are more pronounced than normal. Wide mood swings may be a result of demyelination in the brain or difficulty coping with MS. It is possible for people with MS to have concurrent illnesses such as bipolar disorder or manic depressive illness. An individual who experiences such mood swings needs to be evaluated by a psychologist or psychiatrist who can determine whether the mood swings are a response to the losses and symptoms of MS or to organic causes.

Q: What is the effect of MS on personality and emotions?

A: This is a complex question because demyelination in the brain can cause cognitive, personality, and emotional changes. The person's response to having the disease and her/his response to environmental, family, and job situations can also be factors. One of the major components in dealing with the psychological aspects of MS is the uncertainty of the future. Multiple sclerosis has the potential to be rather devastating, yet it has an unpredictable course. It can be very difficult to deal with this uncertainty. A counselor who is familiar with MS, its psychological component, and techniques for dealing with these things can make a positive impact on the quality of life.

Q: How important is a support group?

A: There has been some phenomenal work in the effect of support groups. Many years ago structured support groups were found helpful for people with MS. More recently, women who were terminally ill with breast cancer were assigned to usual care or to a support group. Those who were in the support group lived for years, whereas those who received standard care without group support died within a few months, as predicted. For some people, however, participating in a group is too stressful, and they would not be advised to do so.

Q: Are the effects of support groups consistent?

A: A lot depends on the structure of the group, the group leader, and the person with MS. Some people are not comfortable talking in a group about anything. For others, a group that allows people to share their knowledge and help each other look at possible ways of coping with what is happening in their lives because of MS can be very helpful. It is not beneficial to sit around and complain about symptoms of multiple sclerosis and other people's response to MS. A group needs a strong leader who can help people look at their coping strategies and develop problem-solving strategies for dealing with what happens in the group.

DISEASE TREATMENTS

In the previous sections, we have answered questions on symptoms and how they can be managed, as well as the management of health, or "wellness" in general. In this section, we answer questions on both conventional and some less conventional therapies.

There is great interest in the multiple sclerosis community about some of the new and encouraging medications that are becoming available. At the time this book went to press, two medications were available for the purpose of altering the course of the disease, Betaseron® (interferon-beta 1b), a medication given subcutaneously every other day, and Avonex® (interferon-beta 1a), given intramuscularly once a week. A third drug, Copaxone® (copolymer or Cop-1), is expected to be available in the near future. Betaseron is very expensive, costing approximately $10,000 a year. However, scientific studies have continued to show beneficial effects of this medication as long as antibodies to it are not developed. Other types of beta interferon will soon be available and other types of medications are being actively studied. The future looks promising for the medical control of MS.

In the past, when no medication was available to alter the course of MS, many people sought alternative medicine. We believe that Western medicine should keep an open mind to some of these techniques. They need to be scientifically studied to be sure that their use does not produce any harm and may indeed have some true benefit. For them to be deemed effective, they need to be shown to work; any improvement that occurs should be shown to be due to the treatment, rather than simply associated with a spontaneous remission or placebo effect.

22

Drugs Affecting the Immune System

As of this writing, two drugs are approved for use in patients that have beneficial effects on the course of the disease, a third should be available shortly, and several others are in more preliminary stages of testing. Because of the rapid changes in this field, we have attempted to provide more basic information on these agents rather than extended details concerning their clinical usage.

Q: What is the length of time between the introduction of a new drug and its use in MS?

A: All new drugs must undergo "clinical trials." These trials are difficult in MS. First of all, the course of MS is extremely variable and large numbers of people must be studied in order to determine whether improvement is brought on by the drug, by some other factor, or by chance. The second problem is the tremendous placebo effect in trials of medications for MS. Someone who has MS may show improvement from the sheer expectation of getting better. Thirdly, bias may occur if the investigator knows that someone is getting an experimental drug. The investigator may "see" improvement in the person that is really not there. Often the effects of drugs are small and difficult to measure. It takes about three years in a multicenter study before sufficient data are available to apply for approval from the Food and

Drug Administration (FDA). The entire process to final approval can be extremely lengthy, but may be speeded up if there is strong evidence that the drug helps and no other effective drugs for the disease are available.

Q: What is being done to overcome the defects in myelin that occur in MS?

A: At present no drug is available that can overcome the defects in myelin. There is, however, exciting research in this field. Intravenous immunoglobulin (IVIg) is being studied as a way to improve conduction in demyelinated nerves. IVIg works by effecting changes in the myelin. Digitalis, which works on the sodium and potassium pump in nerve cells, may be helpful in improving conduction along demyelinated nerves. Other drugs such as 4-aminopyridine (4-AP) and related compounds prolong the action potential along the nerve and enhance conduction. Many agents are now being studied worldwide that have the potential to improve nerve conduction in demyelinated nerves.

Q: Are the lesions in the central nervous system in MS as repairable as nerve damage is in a stroke?

A: Some of the recovery that occurs following a stroke is due to related fields of neurons taking over the functions lost by the stroke. A stroke is usually accompanied by brain swelling; when the swelling subsides, some or all function may be recovered. All of the recovery following a stroke is due to factors other than repair of damaged neurons. In MS there are generally not large areas of damage, and consequently there is not the mass effect of swelling that is common in a stroke, and that type of recovery does not occur.

Q: If nerve cells are not repaired, why do remissions of MS symptoms occur?

A: An MS exacerbation may be caused by acute swelling of focal areas of the central nervous system. This can cause conduction block in these nerves. Corticosteroids can decrease this edema and speed up a remission, but there is no actual repair of demyelinated nerve damage.

Q: Do methylprednisolone and prednisone help?

A: There is general agreement that they should be used only for a short period, during an acute exacerbation. Of the two, intravenous methylprednisolone is the more effective and safer drug.

Q: How effective is high dose IV methylprednisolone in treating exacerbations of MS?

A: Methylprednisolone (Solu-Medrol®) is becoming the accepted treatment for severe exacerbations of MS. It is very important that the exacerbation be treated early. The drug is give intravenously in high doses for three or more days and is followed by a tapering dose of oral corticosteroids over two weeks. This protocol appears to be effective in reducing the severity and duration of an exacerbation. However, it does not affect the long-term course of MS and may not be appropriate for people with the more progressive form of multiple sclerosis.

Q: What results have come from ACTH treatments for MS?

A: ACTH, which stimulates the body's own endogenous steroids, is slightly effective in reducing the severity and duration of exacerbations, but it is not effective in altering the long-term course of MS. As time goes by, MS exacerbations typically become more severe and more frequent, and remissions tend to be less complete, resulting in gradual worsening of residual neurologic deficits.

Q: Can the use of oral prednisone for another medical problem worsen MS symptoms?

A: The use of oral prednisone for any condition can cause serious side effects over time, such as alterations in metabolism, fluid retention, and loss of bone mineral. The adverse effects of long-term steroid therapy must be balanced with the therapeutic effects.

Q: What are immunoglobulins and how are they related to plasmapheresis?

A: Immunoglobulins are antibodies that circulate in the blood. In some cases, they can be "toxic." Plasmapheresis is a technique that removes the toxic antibodies from the blood, but has *not* been shown to be beneficial in MS.

Q: What cancer drugs are used to treat MS?

A: A number of chemotherapeutic agents that are used to treat cancer have also been tried in MS. The most commonly used agents are azathioprine (Imuran®), cyclophosphamide (Cytoxan®), and methotrexate. Unfortunately, these drugs depress the entire immune system, which then makes the person vulnerable to infections. Newer treatments are aimed at modulating parts of the immune system without totally suppressing immunity. In some but not all people, they appear to slow the progressive form of MS.

Q: Are there any treatments for MS directed at the immune system?

A: Many of the treatments that have been tried with MS are based on the knowledge that the immune system seems to be what destroys myelin. Interferons are part of the immune system, and drugs such as beta interferon have been used to modify the immune system.

Q: What is the new drug 2CDA?

A: Cladribine® is the trade name of 2CDA. It is an immune suppressor that is administered by an implanted catheter or by injection. A small initial study suggested that it slows progression in progressive MS. Clinical trials in progressive multiple sclerosis are underway, but it will be years before we know if drugs slow the disease progression.

Q: What has the study of oral myelin produced?

A: A multicenter double blind clinical trial of Myloral®, an oral form of myelin, started in 1994. The study is being conducted at many sites in the United States and Canada, and neither the person with MS nor the researcher knows who is getting the placebo or who is getting oral myelin. It will be some years before we have any information from this research.

Q: Why does so much of what appears about MS treatment focus on beta interferon?

A: Interferons are part of the very complex immune system within the body. Beta interferon is an interferon (the "beta" form) that helps to modulate the way the immune system responds. It reduces the frequency of exacerbations of MS, but it does not prevent all exacerbations. This is a particular benefit to someone who has frequent exacerbations but not as advantageous to someone who only has an exacerbation every year or so, although beta interferon may actually reduce the enlargement of MS lesions and the development of new ones such as identified on MRI scans.

Q: Who should consider taking beta interferon?

A: Beta interferon is now recommended for people who have exacerbating-remitting MS who are able to walk. Other studies have started to test interferons in people with secondary progressive MS and those who are more disabled. People with early or long-standing MS may benefit from taking beta interferon as long as the clinical picture consists of exacerbations and remissions. It is hoped that the reduction in the number of exacerbations also means less cumulative disability.

Q: Is there any evidence that beta interferon is beneficial to someone with progressive MS?

A: Beta interferon has not been approved by the Food and Drug Administration (FDA) for use in either primary or secondary progressive MS. Clinical trials are starting to evaluate beta interferon in other types of MS, but it will be several years before we have answers from those studies. Your local chapter of the National Multiple Sclerosis Society can tell you where those studies are being conducted.

Q: What should I consider in deciding whether or not to use one of the beta interferons or other medications that may become available?

A: Evidence is accumulating that all patients with exacerbating-remitting MS who are ambulatory should seriously consider taking beta interferon. Betaseron® must be taken by injection every other day, while Avonex® can be taken once a week, by an intramuscular injection given by a health care provider. Beta interferon decreases exacerbations only while it is being taken. Some people have undesirable side effects such as skin reactions at the injection site or flu-like symptoms for several months after initiation of therapy. Also, after one to two years of taking it, some patients may develop "blocking antibodies," which may reduce its efficacy in a clinically significant way. These drugs are costly, and some insurance companies may not cover the cost of injectable medications. The vast majority, however, do.

Q: What are the side effects of Betaseron®?

A: Some people have a local reaction of redness and pain at the site of injection. Betaseron® makes some people feel very tired and achy the day they take the injection. It appears that local tissue reactions and the flu-like symptoms diminish over time. It is not uncommon for the white blood cell count to drop or for liver enzymes to rise. Both of these changes return to normal when the drug is stopped. We are learning new ways to prevent side effects. Many and varied symptoms have been attributed to Betaseron® in very small numbers of people using the drug. Often these symptoms are part of MS or are related to another drug the person is taking.

Q: Will the cost of Betaseron® go down?

A: Betaseron® is produced by recombinant DNA, a very expensive technology. There is no reason to suspect that the cost will drop dramatically, although improvement in the manufacturing process and competition from new drugs should result in some cost reductions.

Q: What financial assistance is available for those who cannot afford Betaseron®?

A: Many people with MS have health insurance coverage that does not cover prescription drugs. Contact your local MS Society chapter or the Betaseron Foundation (800-948-5777) for assistance.

Q: What should I expect from beta interferon?

A: The published studies show that beta interferon reduces the frequency and severity of exacerbations in people with relapsing-remitting MS who are still able to walk. Someone who has had four exacerbations a year may find that they have only two exacerbations a year while taking these drugs. There is also evidence from MRI showing less new disease activity.

Q: Does beta interferon relieve symptoms of MS?

A: Beta interferon does not have a direct effect on symptoms such as fatigue, muscle spasms, or the ability to carry out activities of daily living. By decreasing the number of exacerbations and stabilizing lesions in the central nervous system, beta interferon may prevent symptoms from getting worse or new symptoms from appearing, but it will not reverse damage that is already present.

Q: What have we learned from those who have been taking Betaseron®?

A: Betaseron® has been available to people with MS since late 1993, after a very short review process. A "Phase IV" study will collect information from the thousands of people who are using Betaseron®. Our experience has shown that people taking Betaseron® still have exacerbations, but they seem to have a reduction in the exacerbation rate.

Q: How long will I need to take beta interferon?

A: A reasonable analogy is that beta interferon is to multiple sclerosis what insulin is to diabetes. As long as a person with diabetes takes insulin, blood sugar remains in control. As long as a person with MS takes beta interferon, exacerbations remain in control.

Q: Can I stop taking beta interferon?

A: We have experience with people stopping Betaseron® because of inconvenience, because of side effects, or because it did not meet their expectations for decreasing exacerbations. The body does not become dependent on beta interferon, and no general adverse effects have been reported by those who have stopped taking the drug.

Q: Has there been any further research on the effects of gamma interferon?

A: There are three types of interferon: alpha, beta, and gamma. Initially, gamma interferon looked the most promising. It had been used in patients with cancer. However, MS symptoms worsened in at least two clinical trials. It is no longer being studied for MS. Interferon alpha is currently being studied and may be effective as a treatment for MS.

Q: What does the future hold?

A: Studies are being planned to evaluate the effect of beta interferon on secondary progressive MS. Other studies will explore different dosage schedules and combining beta interferon with other drugs. Avonex®, a beta interferon that needs to be injected into a muscle once a week, has just become available. As people with MS continue to use beta interferon for many years, we will learn about the long-term positive and negative effects of the drug.

Q: What is Cop-1?

A: Copolymer-1 (Cop-1) is a synthetic polypeptide that is being used to stimulate immune tolerance in the body. It is immunologically cross-reactive with myelin basic protein and may promote the development of antigen-specific suppressor T-cells. Human trials of Cop-1 suggest a decrease in rate of relapse. At the time of this writing, it is expected that the drug will soon be available in the United States under the trade name Copaxone®.

Q: What do you mean by a "placebo effect?"

A: A placebo is a "sugar pill"—an inert substance that the person taking it feels is an active medication. Because of the person's belief that it is of medicinal value, the patient gets better. This can be a powerful effect and greatly complicates research on the effect of drugs for MS. Often people receiving a placebo even report side effects identical to those of the active drug.

Q: How do over-the-counter antihistamines and other allergy medicines affect MS?

A: Antihistamines do not affect the underlying course of MS. They may, however, temporarily worsen symptoms of MS, including fatigue and bladder dysfunction.

Alternative Therapies

Q: Is there any indication that acupuncture is helpful for MS?

A: There is much about acupuncture that we do not understand clearly. It seems to be beneficial for some symptoms of MS, particularly pain. There is no strong evidence that it alters other symptoms, such as bladder dysfunction.

Q: Is hypnosis ever used in the treatment of MS, in particular for anxiety attacks?

A: Many symptomatic benefits have been attributed to hypnosis, but it does not alter the course of the disease. A good operating principle is to look at the cost:benefit ratio. If it does not cost too much in terms of money, time, and energy to undergo hypnosis, it may be worth the investment to see if it helps.

Q: What is known about shiatsu therapy and acupressure and their effect on fatigue in MS?

A: We do not understand the physiology of how things like shiatsu and acupressure work. We do know that some people find them effective, particularly for treating specific symptoms such as muscle spasticity or pain. It is more difficult to treat a global symptom such as fatigue with these strategies, although they often have a very relaxing effect which, indeed, can help lessen fatigue.

Q: Can chiropractic therapy help symptoms of MS?

A: Multiple sclerosis is a disease of the brain and spinal cord. From that perspective, chiropractic techniques have no place in treating the disease itself. Symptomatic relief of secondary symptoms of MS, such as contractures of limbs, muscle pain, and other musculoskeletal symptoms, may be helped by chiropractic manipulations, physical therapy treatments, or other types of treatments directed to the musculoskeletal system.

Q: Can a chiropractor lessen strain on limbs that are affected by MS?

A: The maintenance of health in a person with MS is a very complex and interactive issue. People with MS can have the same variety of soft tissue problems as people without MS. People with MS may have decreased muscle strength, which makes them more prone to such things as sprains, strains, and other types of soft tissue injuries. A variety of health care providers, including a medical doctor, doctor of osteopathy, or chiropractor can lessen these problems. It is important to find a practitioner who is qualified and experienced in the specific problem and who understands MS.

Q: Can massage therapy be helpful for the person with MS?

A: Massage *feels* very good. Although it has no effect on the course of MS, massage can help loosen tight tissues. It also increases blood flow to the tissues, and increased blood flow itself has healing qualities. Muscle tightness because of spasticity, inactivity, or other problems with MS can be helped by massage, and joint mobility can be improved.

Q: Can massage therapy alleviate pain in MS?

A: Massage therapy is one of those strategies that works well for some people's pain but not for others. The underlying cause of the pain is probably what predicts when massage helps. Massage is a relatively low cost intervention with fewer side effects than drugs and certainly can be tried to alleviate pain.

Q: Are there any studies with MS patients that show the effect of visualization or autosuggestion on the immune system?

A: There have been many studies on the effect of cognitive therapies such as visualization and similar types of interventions on the immune system. Although we are not aware of any study in this area that has focused on MS, there have been people with MS included in some of the studies. Those strategies do have a positive effect on the immune system and may be worth trying.

Q: What other effects does guided imagery and meditation have?

A: Guided imagery, meditation, and similar cognitive strategies are very beneficial. They help decrease the stress levels by altering the way in which the person responds to stressors. These strategies are not for everyone. Some do much better dealing with stress and improving well-being by running a marathon.

Q: Can biofeedback help the person with MS?

A: Biofeedback is most effective in teaching a person to reduce levels of muscle tension that are associated with certain types of pain, such as muscle tension headaches. Biofeedback also has been tried in MS with regard to managing spasticity or muscle tension states. A number of studies looking at EMG biofeedback in people with MS have shown that biofeedback is less effective in managing spasticity than it is for pain related to muscle tension.

Q: What are the benefits of Tai Chi in someone with MS?

A: Tai Chi is a martial art that utilizes force in a therapeutic way. Martial arts will not prevent the progression of demyelination but they have very beneficial effects on the body. Tai Chi focuses on the economic use of energy, strengthens cardiovascular capacity, improves digestion, balances energy, and results in a dynamic feeling of health, increases muscle tone, strength, and flexibility. It improves coordination, physical agility, and speed. Tai Chi helps to transcend internal or external obstacles so it results in a feeling of focus in daily life, increased self-esteem and self-discipline. Practitioners report harmony of mind and body, a positive manner toward life and self, and a greater respect for self and others.

Q: Are there any studies going on for bee sting therapy for MS?

A: Yes, at least two current ones. Neither has yet published data. Bee stings have been suggested as a way to enhance the immune system in people with MS. Currently, there is no scientific proof that these are effective.

Q: What is the benefit of hyperbaric oxygen (HBO) in MS?

A: This is an interesting issue. A decade ago there was a paper in the *New England Journal of Medicine* which suggested that hyperbaric oxygen was helpful in MS. Other centers tried to reproduce this and were unable to obtain beneficial effects. For example, we did a study on HBO in which we measured such things as the ability of a person to walk in a straight line, the ability to walk quickly, and hand function, using a variety of measurements. We were initially very impressed with the benefits of HBO, but the problem was that people learned how to take the test—they simply got better at taking the evaluating test by retaking it. This is something that makes MS research so difficult. The current medical opinion is that hyperbaric oxygen is not effective in MS and does not have a role in the treatment of MS.

Q: Are scientists studying treatment options such as evening primrose oil, flax seed oil, or Lorenzo's oil?

A: Many, many treatments have been suggested for MS that are thought to be capable of altering the immune system. There has been little research done on these substances as treatments for MS. Although some people have anecdotally reported improvement, it is not possible to sort out how much change in their MS was due to the placebo effect. Lorenzo's oil is aimed at metabolic defect and is not appropriate for people with MS.

Q: Would smoking marijuana on a daily basis help guard against the stress and pain related to MS?

A: The active ingredient in marijuana has been shown to decrease the nausea associated with cancer chemotherapy. There have also been anecdotal reports of marijuana decreasing spasticity. However, small doses of marijuana impair simple motor tasks, reactions times, and short-term memory. Driving performance has been shown to be impaired for four to eight hours. Chronic use of marijuana has been implicated in decreased motivation, loss of effectiveness, impaired judgment, concentration, memory, and communication skills, as well as the inability to set goals and manage stress. Marijuana is an illegal substance in the United States, and its use can result in additional neurologic symptoms.

Health Care Team

Q: At what point should a person consult a physical therapist?

A: A physical therapist can help design an exercise program that is specific to an individual's needs early in the course of MS. Even people with minimal disability can benefit from suggestions about physical activity. It is best not to wait until symptoms are severe before getting help. Reevaluation by a physical therapist is appropriate when there has been a change in functional ability and a new activity or exercise program may be indicated.

Q: Are there any specialized training or credentialing standards for physical therapists treating people with MS?

A: Physical therapy schools are increasingly recognizing the important role that physical therapy has in the management of people with MS, and physical therapists are active participants in such organizations as the Consortium of Multiple Sclerosis Centers. There are increasing numbers of postgraduate and continuing education programs for therapists to learn about MS. However, there are no credentialing standards specific for MS.

Q: Does the National Multiple Sclerosis Society have guidelines for physical therapists caring for people with MS?

A: The NMSS does not have specific guidelines for physical therapists. However, the NMSS is very concerned about providing necessary information for people with MS. They have educational materials on exercises in MS that have been reviewed and approved by experts. However, caution is necessary in applying these materials to individuals because what is good for one person may be too much or too vigorous for another. Exercise must be individualized for each person.

Q: Who should be included on a health care team for someone with MS?

A: The person with MS is a critical part of the health care team and needs to be involved in planning management strategies. The signs and symptoms of MS dictate who else is needed on the team. Certainly someone who can take care of your general health is essential. This might be a primary care physician, an internist, or a nurse practitioner. A neurologist or MS specialist may be needed to manage the medical treatment and acute exacerbations of MS. A counselor, psychologist, or psychiatrist can help the person with MS and family members to cope with depression or cognitive problems of MS. A physiatrist or physical therapist can address problems of physical function and activities of daily living. An occupational therapist, vocational counselor, and speech pathologist are also important members of the health care team. A urologist or nurse specialist can address bladder problems. A social worker can identify resources available to help the person with MS. Each health care team needs to be individualized and may draw on a wide variety of specialists.

Q: How can people in rural areas contact specialists in MS?

A: There are a number of Multiple Sclerosis Clinical Centers in the country, and many are associated with schools of medicine that can provide consultation to physicians in rural areas. The local chapter of the National Multiple Sclerosis Society can identify the nearest resources.

Q: How can someone with MS be sure of receiving quality health care?

A: The person with MS is truly the expert in the effect that MS is having on them and with respect to what things help and do not help. The National Multiple Sclerosis Society publishes newsletters and literature that update people about current treatments for the disease itself and symptoms of MS. It is incumbent on each individual with MS to be as informed about the disease and to bring information as well as questions to health care professionals. The most important question to be answered is whether MS and its symptoms are being addressed adequately and comprehensively by the health care providers and the person with MS.

SOCIAL ASPECTS

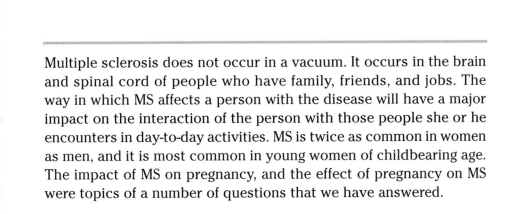

Multiple sclerosis does not occur in a vacuum. It occurs in the brain and spinal cord of people who have family, friends, and jobs. The way in which MS affects a person with the disease will have a major impact on the interaction of the person with those people she or he encounters in day-to-day activities. MS is twice as common in women as men, and it is most common in young women of childbearing age. The impact of MS on pregnancy, and the effect of pregnancy on MS were topics of a number of questions that we have answered.

Family Relationships

Q: What advice do you have for family members dealing with MS?

A: Multiple sclerosis is truly a disease that affects all members of a family. Just as MS differs from one person to another, families also differ. That makes it difficult to make hard and fast recommendations to families. Probably the most important thing is for family members to maintain open communication about the issues related to MS, to be able to talk about those issues, and to jointly solve problems relating to those issues.

Q: How do you go about involving loved ones in an active wellness program?

A: Wellness is not a solitary activity. It is one that involves the other people in the living environment. People who are part of developing a program are more likely to participate than they would be if they were just told what to do. To develop a wellness program, you probably need to work with a primary health care provider who can address all aspects of health promotion and disease prevention. Diet, exercise, and sleep are just as important as screening for major illness. Developing a wellness program requires that everyone in the family talk about their priorities and how they are going to manage to such things as diet, exercise, sleep, and stress.

Q: Why do people withdraw from someone who is diagnosed with MS?

A: The issue of people isolating themselves from someone with MS, or any chronic illness or disability, is a real problem that occurs too frequently. Often people isolate themselves because they do not understand what is going on; they are frightened because they cannot stop the progression of the disease in someone they love. Illness in someone close often makes people feel vulnerable to illness themselves. The person with MS who needs to change her/his level of participation in recreational activities may find friends withdraw because they want things to continue as they had been.

Q: What can you do with family and friends who isolate themselves from you when you get MS?

A: A lot of what a person with MS can do when feeling isolated depends on the relationship with the other person prior to diagnosis. Communication is an important part of dealing with that. If you have never been able to communicate well, it will be even more difficult to communicate now that MS is in the picture. Meet people person-to-person on an individual level to communicate about MS and how it is affecting you. Reassure them that nothing they did caused the disease. Help them look at how they can relate to you as a person, not as someone who is sick or disabled.

Q: What will help family members cope with changes in lifestyle after an exacerbation?

A: Communication is critical in helping family members cope with change caused by MS. It is important for the person with MS to talk about what is different in her life, what she is no longer able to do, and to negotiate with other family members about how those things will get done. Looking at how you communicate and having some dialogue and sharing helps family members understand what is going on. Many of the symptoms of MS are invisible ("hidden disability") and family members are dependent on the person with MS to tell them when a problem occurs. Sometimes taking the opportunity to talk with other people who have a family member with MS or with a counselor is very helpful.

Sexuality

Q: Can the disease process of MS itself cause a decrease in sex drive?

A: Sex drive is a very complex phenomenon. It is a state of mind that can be affected by many things, including self-image and emotions. Physical changes that are caused by MS can also affect sex drive. MS can affect the nerve pathways that are important for the physiological responses associated with sexual activity. Damage to sensory pathways can decrease or make painful previously comfortable sensations associated with intercourse. Muscle spasms in the legs can create problems, especially for women. Drugs used to treat symptoms of MS can blunt the sex drive. Damaged myelin cannot be replaced but there are many things that can be done to work around specific problems. A counselor can help work through the emotional issues that may decrease sex drive.

Q: Is sexual dysfunction in MS ever psychological?

A: A major contributor to sexual performance is how people see themselves as men or women. Feelings of attractiveness can be altered because of physical disability caused by MS. Sometimes people feel that they cannot be a good sexual partner because they have MS.

The belief that you cannot have a good intimate relationship tends to become a "self-fulfilling prophecy."

Q: What resources are available to deal with sexual problems?

A: The first and foremost is open communication. Talk to your partner about what is going on. Self-help books are available that cover all aspects of intimate relationships. Do not be afraid to seek professional help from your personal health care provider or a marriage and family counselor.

Pregnancy and Menopause

Q: How does childbearing affect MS?

A: We know that most women with MS do very well during pregnancy, but may have an exacerbation of neurologic symptoms during the six to twelve months following delivery. We have no way to predict who will have an exacerbation following delivery of a child, but we do know that pregnancy has no long-term effect on the progression of MS.

Q: What are the chances of passing MS on to my children?

A: Multiple sclerosis tends to occur a bit more frequently in families than in the general population, but it is not a genetically inherited disease. There is, however, a genetic predisposition that makes it more likely that people whose near relatives have MS and who have other, as yet unknown, factors will develop MS. About one in one hundred children of a parent with MS will develop the disease.

Q: What advice do you have for a woman who is pregnant?

A: It is best to be prepared for the worst case scenario, and having some support systems in place prior to your child's birth is certainly good insurance. If you do not need those support services, great! Planning ahead insures that you will not be in a panic situation trying to find resources that you need in a crisis. However, the most important question for each woman with MS who is considering a pregnancy to answer is whether she is physically and emotionally able to care for the child. (For more information on this topic, interested readers may want to consult *Mother To Be: A Guide to Pregnancy and Birth for Women with Disabilities* by Judith Rogers and Molleen Matsumura. New York: Demos, 1991.)

Q: What things should I consider in deciding to have a child?

A: This is a complicated issue for everyone, with some added features if a parent has MS. The course that the MS is following needs to be added to the equation about having children. Raising children is a difficult emotional and physical task as well as a financial commitment. Physical care of a child can present challenges to a parent with a physical disability. Asking "what if..." questions and preparing for the worst can ease the role of parenthood. "What if one parent is no longer able to contribute to the work of the family?" "What if a parent is unable to maintain full-time employment?" "What if a parent becomes physically or cognitively disabled?" Knowing your options for coping ahead of time is good insurance that, like all insurance, you hope you never need to use.

Q: Can the hormonal changes that occur during menopause exacerbate MS?

A: We do not have any evidence that the normal hormonal changes that occur during menopause exacerbate MS. However, many of the symptoms of menopause are not unlike some of the symptoms of MS. Probably the best management of those symptoms is hormonal replacement with both estrogen (Premarin®) and progesterone (Provera®). Estrogen helps to manage those symptoms by replacing the estrogen no longer produced by the women's body, and the progesterone decreases the risk of developing uterine cancer that is associated with estrogen alone.

VII

FINANCIAL BURDEN

We have said in the preceding section on social aspects that MS does not occur in a vacuum. It occurs in a person who has a family and friends. Frequently, the affected person also has a job. The disease can affect employment and, consequently, income.

Not only may MS affect income negatively, with the advent of expensive new medications the costs of care have skyrocketed. This can result in an economic "double whammy" for the person with MS. At the present time, Betaseron® costs approximately $10,000 per year. Although in some cases insurance covers this entirely, in most cases insurance covers medications with a co-payment, which could mean that a patient may have to pay as much as several hundred dollars per month for this medication. A person with MS on Medicare has an even greater problem since Medicare does not cover the cost of medication. This may mean that the person with MS who must rely on Medicare may, in reality, not have access to drugs that reduce the progression of the disease. For these people, such a medication might as well not exist. Because of costs of medications and care, as well as the negative impact on employment and the long duration of the disease, financial matters are of great consequence for people with MS.

Insurance

Q: What can we do to get Medicare to pay for new drug therapies?

A: Medicare does not pay for most medications. Medicare is a federal program that may serve as a model for any new national health care plan. Contact your congressional and senatorial representatives and let them know the importance of including benefits for treatment of chronic diseases such as MS in any new plans that are proposed.

Q: Is there anything that can be done to get insurance companies to pay for more physical therapy?

A: Most insurance companies are willing to reimburse for short-term therapy programs when they can see measurable improvement. In a progressive disease such as MS, "improvement" may actually be a retardation of progression, although improvement is always the goal. As we look at major changes in the health care system in the United States, write to your employer, insurance company, as well as your congressional representatives and senators and explain your needs in terms of health care coverage and why it is important for those needs to be included in new benefit packages.

Q: What kinds of programs are available to help with the cost of medications?

A: Many insurance plans, Medicare among them, do not pay for most drugs taken at home. Even when the policy covers a percentage of drug costs, the remaining portion can be substantial. Many pharmaceutical companies have programs that help defray the cost of their products. Check with your health care provider who prescribed the medication for more information.

Q: Are there any insurance companies that will take a person with MS?

A: The issue of insurance for someone with MS is a recurrent concern. There are many insurance policies that exclude preexisting conditions when writing a new policy. With health care reform, some states have already made it illegal to exclude preexisting conditions. Health care and life insurance policies are available for people with chronic diseases such as MS. These policies often cost more because the actuarial data show that people with long-term illness use certain services more than people without a health problem.

Appendix A
Exercise Videos

Keep Fit While You Sleep (1992)
Suggested audience: Persons who use wheelchairs
(Note: film contains product advertising)
VHS 1/2 inch

ORDER FROM:
Twin Peaks Press
P.O. Box 129
Vancouver, WA 98666
800-637-2256
$29.95 + $4.50 handling

The MS Workout
Suggested audience: Persons who are ambulatory without aids
VHS 1/2 inch

ORDER FROM:
National Multiple Sclerosis Society
New York City Chapter
30 West 26th Street
New York, NY 10010
212-463-7787
$15.00

The Wheelchair Workout
Suggested audience: Persons who use wheelchairs
VHS 1/2 inch

ORDER FROM:
National Multiple Sclerosis Society
New York City Chapter
30 West 26th Street
New York, NY 10010
212-463-7787
$15.00

Armchair Fitness

Suggested audience: Range from persons who are ambulatory to those who use wheelchairs
VHS 1/2 inch; 60 minutes

ORDER FROM:
CC-M Productions
8510 Cedar Street
Silver Spring, MS 20910
800-453-6280
$39.95 + $2.50 handling

Nancy's Special Workout

Suggested audience: People with MS, polio, spina bifida, etc.
VHS 1/2 inch; 45 minutes

ORDER FROM:
Nancy's Special Workout
P.O. Box 2914
Southfield, MI 48037
313-682-5511
$39.95

Theracise

Suggested audience: Persons with upper extremity disability
VHS 1/2 inch; 30 minutes

ORDER FROM:
Thera Cise, Inc.
P.O. Box 9100, Unit 107
Newton Center, MA 02159
617-332-6160
$34.95 + $2.00 shipping and handling

⌖Appendix B⌖

A Guide to Daily Food Choices

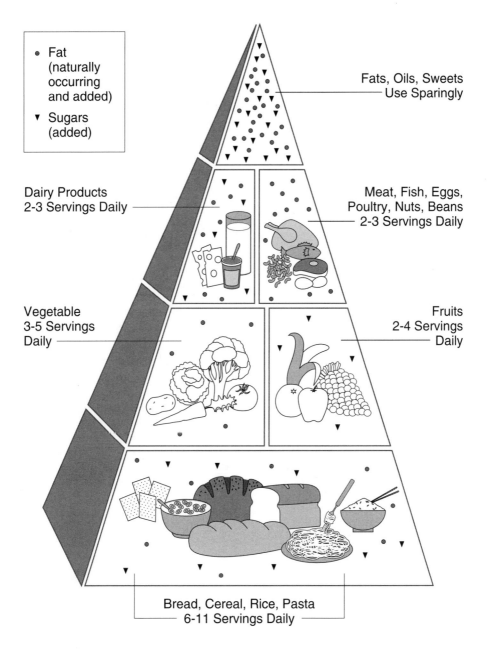

- Fat (naturally occurring and added)
- ▼ Sugars (added)

Fats, Oils, Sweets
Use Sparingly

Dairy Products
2-3 Servings Daily

Meat, Fish, Eggs,
Poultry, Nuts, Beans
2-3 Servings Daily

Vegetable
3-5 Servings
Daily

Fruits
2-4 Servings
Daily

Bread, Cereal, Rice, Pasta
6-11 Servings Daily

Source: U.S. Department of Agriculture/U.S. Department of Health and Human Services

☙Index☙